CW01011040

How Did We End Up Here?

Surviving and Thriving in a Character-Disordered World

George K. Simon Jr., Ph.D.

with

M. Kathryn Armistead, Ph.D.

Books by George K. Simon Jr., Ph.D.

In Sheep's Clothing: Understanding and Dealing with Manipulative People, Revised Edition

Character Disturbance: The Phenomenon of Our Age

The Judas Syndrome: Why Good People Do Awful Things

Dedication

This book is dedicated to the many avid followers of my manipulative-people.com blog, whose insightful comments and faithful devotion have always inspired my work, and to those individuals who take the cause of character seriously and willingly accept the burdens that come with forging a life of integrity and responsibility.

Acknowledgements

This book would not have been possible without the vision, dedication, and remarkable creative talent of Kathy Armistead. I'm blessed beyond measure to have been the beneficiary of her understanding, support, zeal, and ability to present my perspectives in a most readable manner.

I'm also grateful to the thousands of individuals who have read my books, reviewed my blog articles, or come across my work in some other way and have contacted me to share their appreciation and their stories. I treasure the wisdom and validation they've given me and hope this book reflects the value of their contributions.

Perhaps I'm most indebted to my wife of thirty-five years, Sherry, and to my wonderful children and grandchildren, who provide living proof on a daily basis of how much character matters and constantly inspire me to be a better person.

Contents

Introduction
How Did We End Up Here?

Do you sometimes wonder how you ended up where you are now? How the relationship that once seemed to hold such promise went so terribly wrong? Perhaps you even wonder how we ended up where we are as a society — so many dysfunctional relationships. Maybe you're at the end of the road. Or maybe you're in the midst of a troubling situation, trying to decide what to do. In any case, you want to understand what's happened and why. Whether there's any hope. How you can pick up the pieces and move forward. And most of all, how you can avoid a similar fate in the future.

If you are in a relationship with someone who hurts, manipulates, or belittles you, there's a good chance that you're not happy and that something is missing. Or maybe you're involved with a person who is just hard to live with, who is demanding and unforgiving of even the slightest mistakes. And while you might not be significantly unhappy or even depressed, you may still find yourself searching for a more fulfilling and satisfying existence. It could be that you are in a relationship with a person with a disturbed or disordered character. If you are, you know that their behavior is often baffling and confusing. "Why does he get upset over something so small?" you ask yourself. Or "Why doesn't he just tell me the truth?" "Why does she always have to win and control everybody else?" "Why is everything that goes wrong my fault?" If you find yourself asking these questions, if you find that these troubled people present you with seemingly intractable relational issues, that their behavior is a hard to understand, this book can help you. Here you will find practical answers to these questions:

Am I dealing with a disturbed character?

How can I effectively confront and deal with the problems they cause?

Is a better relationship possible?

How can I assess the potential for change?

Should I stay or just let go?

In fact, it may not even matter why you are here. The fact is that you are. And what matters is that things need to change and get better. What would it take for you to truly be happy in your relationships? Are you willing to face up to the issues and seek change? Don't give up. There is hope even in a character-disturbed world. Disturbed characters don't have to call the shots. You don't have to "settle." Instead you can thrive, make better decisions, and move on if that's what you decide to do. This book can show you how.

**

As the leading authority on manipulative people, I have spent over twenty-five years as a clinical psychologist and consultant working and studying persons with disturbed characters and their victims. With this book's practical approach and empowerment tools found in each chapter, you will find the help you need to deal with these disturbed characters. After all, we all want to be happier and enjoy healthier relationships.

Character and the Science of Happiness

A refreshing avenue of research has emerged in the mental health field: the science of happiness. It is positive and forward-looking. But there are some detractors. That's largely because one of its major tenets is that various aspects of a person's character are key to happiness. The word "character" derives from both the Old French and Greek words meaning to engrave or furrow a *distinctive mark*. The word has been used to denote the most distinguishing traits of overall personality that uniquely define or mark an individual as a social being. Most especially, the term commonly reflects an individual's positive personality aspects—those socially desirable qualities and virtues such as self-control, ethical behavior, loyalty, and fortitude. A well developed, mature character is something to which we should all aspire.

A person with a mature healthy character has at least six basic characteristics.

1. The people with the kind of mature character we talk about in this book do not need to hurt an opponent unnecessarily and aggression subsides when the goal in question is reached. This is opposed to immature people who exhibit hatred and cruelty in the elimination of human obstacles to achieve a goal.

2. Mature characters enter into interpersonal relationships for mutual joy and fulfillment, not merely for a personal satisfaction of pleasure.

3. Mature characters become increasingly objective vis-à-vis their self, their problems, and the problems of others.

4. Mature characters experience joyful pride and creative achievement in significant relationships that continue to deepen and broaden in scope.

5. Mature characters can give and receive empathic response to and from others without threatening their own self-boundaries.

6. Mature characters are usually altruistic. They are committed to selfless, humanistic behavior, not rooted in the pangs of guilt or in an unacknowledged selfish desire for admiration or immortal reputation. These people feely and completely commit themselves to advancing the greater good. They are not "neurotic" because they have no driving desire to avoid guilt or shame for doing otherwise. They are not out for personal glory or to be revered by society, and they simply and nobly choose to subordinate their own selfish desires for

the good of all. And while none of us are perfect, nevertheless, we walk this path.

However, drawing attention to character issues that might contribute to behavioral problems, emotional disturbances, and other psychological maladies has never been popular in the professional community. That's because of the fear that a treatment provider might overly weight the role of personal responsibility and discount the role of biological and environmental factors in the problems and unhappiness of their client. But the science of happiness is not about indicting people for the deficiencies in their character that might negatively impact their happiness. Rather, it seeks to help people cultivate the characteristics that foster happiness and develop the resources and strength of character necessary to better weather the storms of life. And in scientifically exploring the various factors that influence happiness, we can learn what skills folks need to acquire in order to attain and sustain happiness.

The Capacity to Learn and Adapt

While I'm a fan of this science, I'm also a big fan of these distinguishing features of being human: the incredible capacities to learn and adapt—change. Regardless of our biology, our upbringing, or the nature of circumstances, we can always learn new and better ways to cope and prosper. And it's primarily because of these powerful capacities that we can approach the future with hope and confidence. But, of course, some people pursue happiness in such a self-centered, hedonistic, and callous way that they actually end up making, not only themselves, but others around them quite miserable. Other personalities are so inherently fearful of self-assertion and overly dependent upon unreliable sources of external support that true happiness eludes them most of their lives. But all of us can learn to examine and modify our core beliefs, attitudes, and behavior patterns. We can hone new skills. We can stretch ourselves and improve those socially desirable qualities and virtues such as self-control, ethical behavior, loyalty, and fortitude. But for us to improve our character, we may have to confront our own demons and perhaps the disturbed characters in our lives. In order to be happy and healthy, we may have to initiate change by confronting those who cause us grief.

The Importance of Character in Today's World

Character is shaped in large measure by the kinds of beliefs we come to hold about the nature of the world around us and how best to deal with it. Recently there have been some particularly insidious ideologies spreading across the globe — ideologies, which those who feel disenfranchised in one way or another, unfortunately find all too attractive. Such ideologies have visited us before, and when those who were attracted to them for one reason or another embraced them and rose to power, the results were catastrophic—witness the "master race" ideology of Nazi Germany, for example. So when a troubled character embraces a way of thinking—especially one that not only allows but lauds the deliberate victimization of those who don't adhere to that same way of thinking, it should give us great pause.

With the continued spread of ideologies that promote hate, prejudice, and injustice, we must be especially vigilant when we experience the effects of troubled thinking in our own relationships. It's an ominous and potentially apocalyptic elephant in our midst. And if we don't recognize it honestly and deal directly with both the ideology and the factors that lead some misguided souls to embrace it so eagerly, civil society is likely to be trampled in the impending stampede. But not just in the broader culture, because this kind of person can be part of our own sphere of influence. And it can be up to us to stop them before they go too far down the road of destruction.

These are people we read about and see on the news, and we may be living with one ourselves. These people have to be confronted if we want anything to change, and sometimes one confrontation is not enough. But there are better and worse ways, more effective and less effective ways to confront. This book will give you the tools you need to help you confront the troubling individuals in your life.

Character Determines How We Act

People across the country were at once stunned and horrified when a man entered a food processing facility in Moore, Oklahoma — a town still recovering from a devastating tornado the previous year — and brutally attacked a woman at random, stabbing her repeatedly and then gruesomely decapitating her. The assailant was in the process of stabbing yet another victim when the chief operating officer of the company, who just happened to also be a reserve Sheriff's officer and who happened to be armed, shot him and thwarted a possible second beheading. As tragic as the event was, it has a lot to teach us not only about what's behind so many of the social nightmares we experience these days, but also why it's so imperative that we abandon some of the misguided notions about how these problems can be solved.

Alton Nolen had just been fired from Vaughn Foods for a variety of undisclosed personnel issues. Workers told reporters that he had been trying to convert his co-workers to his religion and making statements about the dire fate that awaits all non-believers. And if Nolen's actions and the actions of other individuals harboring the same disturbing ideology should teach us anything at all, they should teach us that *what we think and believe really matters*, because that thinking is so inextricably linked to how we behave.

Psychology has undergone a sort of revolution over the past few decades, and some prefer to call it the Cognitive-Behavioral revolution (the revolution that gave birth to cognitive-behavioral therapy or CBT). Whereas in times past professionals mainly concerned themselves with the kinds of unconscious emotional conflicts that could make a person "neurotic" or sick with worry and anxiety, more often than not these days professionals turn their attention to the kinds of thinking and beliefs people hold that predispose them to behave in socially problematic ways.

These problem characters fall into two general categories:

1. Those who say all kinds of ridiculous things to explain (i.e., rationalize, attempt to justify) their irresponsible behavior. These are the folks who have you to scratching your head and asking yourself: "Do they really believe the crazy stuff they're spouting?"

2. Those individuals who sincerely embrace some warped and twisted thinking.

The people in the second group are far more dangerous than the first because of their twisted thinking. "Twisted thinking" is always at the root of a person's character disturbance. People who have a distorted take on reality often really know better at some level. Such folks often say crazy things, not so much because they truly believe them but because they want *you* to believe they think that way. They don't want to reveal their real motivations or agendas. But when someone actually holds a twisted set of beliefs, and especially when they hold them with disturbing conviction, it's pretty much inevitable that they will do something horrifying one day.

The incident in Moore should make some things abundantly clear to us: disturbed characters always have and will use just about anything they can think of to accomplish their nefarious ends. Passing tougher laws and imposing greater penalties won't solve the problem. That's because, for the most part, our problems lie in the hearts of people, and only people who are reasonably good-hearted and conscientious pay attention to the rules anyway. So, what do we do with disturbed characters who harbor attitudes, beliefs, and ways of thinking that predispose them to behave irresponsibly at best and in lethally dangerous ways at worst? That is the greatest challenge of our time.

Personality Can Open Doors but Character Keeps Them Open

Many people confuse "personality" and "character." Elmer Letterman is purported to have said "Personality can open doors, but only character can keep them open." The claim makes the point that although one's personality or "style" of relating to others can be of such a quality as to be quite attractive and engaging, especially with a first impression, only those virtuous aspects of one's character, such as integrity, honesty, and commitment to right conduct will ultimately earn the enduring respect, trust, and support of others.

The importance of character has been known for centuries. The ancient Greek, Heraclitus, proclaimed that "a man's character is his fate." And thinkers such as Ralph Waldo Emerson underscore the important role character plays in how a person both views and deals with the world has been Emerson said: "People seem not to see that their opinion of the world is also a confession of their character." He also said, "Character is higher than intellect... A great soul will be strong to live, as well as to think." (See Ralph Waldo Emerson. Essays: Second Series, *Essay Three: Character* [1844].)

Character also tempers the way people use power. I have long challenged the notion that power is an inevitable corruptor of character. There is no power greater than the power a parent has over an infant child in its utter, helpless early dependency. Still, most parents of decent character approach such a position with a deep sense of awe and trepidation, careful to wield the power they hold with great care and noble purpose, sacrificing and nurturing as opposed to self-aggrandizing or abusing. That's why I subscribe to the belief that one's attitude toward the use of power defines one's character better than any other quality. Abraham Lincoln may have said it best: "Nearly all men can stand adversity, but if you want to test a man's character, give him power." In my experience, persons of troubled character tend to seek power ravenously and almost always abuse it when they acquire it.

As a testament to the noble cause of character development, and to the effort and commitment it takes to accomplish the task, English historian, James A. Froude proclaimed: "You cannot dream yourself into a character; you must hammer and forge yourself into one." Developing sound character takes work—a lot of work. And as difficult as it is, instilling controls upon one's baser instincts is the easier part of it; but with determined practice, one can develop virtues. But to develop virtues, you have to practice them and that means an honest self-reckoning: examining one's conscience as well as one's track record of performance, especially under adversity. As Helen Keller once said: "Character cannot be developed in ease and quiet. Only through experience of trial and suffering can the soul be strengthened, vision cleared, ambition inspired, and success achieved."

People of Character Make a Difference

Surely you have heard about Malala Yousafzai. Malala is the young Pashtun woman from the Swat Valley area of Pakistan, who, at seventeen, is the youngest person to win the Nobel Peace Prize. She continues to make history as a tireless advocate for women's rights. You may remember that when Malala was fifteen, a Taliban gunman boarded the school bus she was riding, asked for her by name, then shot her three times, critically injuring her. Both she and her father, who operates a chain of schools in the Swat region, had received death threats from the extremists because their advocacy of women's educational rights. Since the age of twelve Malala had been writing a blog under a pseudonym; and despite the risk she knew she faced for doing so, Malala felt compelled to speak out on the principles of equality and justice. Despite miraculously surviving the attempt on her life and the continued threats, Malala uses the notoriety she has gained and the resources she has earned, including those have come her way from the publication of a book about her ordeal, to work as an advocate to champion women's issues worldwide. This exceptional young woman is truly an inspiration to many and a living testament to the importance and power of character.

While there may be few who have had to face adversity like Malala, there are many people who, despite incredible odds, provide living proof of the power of the human spirit. These individuals not only made deep impressions but also taught me a great deal. Perhaps the most important thing they taught me is how much character really does matter. I'm not just talking about tenacity in the face of adversity. If tenacity itself were the mark of great character, then all the stubbornly steadfast criminals, who persist in their dysfunctional ways of thinking and their problematic conduct would be heroes. Instead, I'm talking about unwavering devotion to *principle* — a devotion so strong that a person is willing to stand up for that principle even when the price tag for doing so becomes unthinkably high.[1]

---

[1] **Note to Reader:** Willingness to stand on principle doesn't mean that one is unnecessarily dogmatic and unyielding. It is the mark of a mature, sound character to be flexible when appropriate and make a place for mercy and compromise. A mature character also has balance what is best for himself with what is best for others and deal with inevitable exceptions while, at the same time, being true to one's convictions.

Bad Circumstances Don't Make People Bad

Individuals with character have also taught me that bad circumstances and abusive treatment by others don't automatically cause someone to become a bad person. I've had the privilege of encountering individual after individual who came from the most abusive and impoverished backgrounds and experienced traumas more horrendous than anyone could possibly imagine, yet they somehow managed to become persons of enviable character. Bad circumstances just don't automatically make people behave badly because of impaired characters. It's not that simple. Poor character is more often the result of things that *don't* happen in a person's life that really need to happen if they're to develop integrity, and even more often, it is the result of toxic beliefs and attitudes the individual forms. What and how we think is important. What we're taught to value matters too, especially how we value those different from us with empathy.

Nurturing empathy for others is essential for character formation. Those who have learned to think about themselves and the world around them in both a positive and principled way often develop the kind character that allows them to remain decent, even in the face of great adversity. Character can be likened to a psychological "immune system," because it insulates a person against the "slings and arrows" and the many negative influences, which we need if we work to make the world a better place. Malala has been quoted as saying that "when the whole world is silent, even one voice becomes powerful." Truer words were never spoken. Martin Luther King Jr., Mahatma Gandhi, Susan B. Anthony, Mother Theresa—they all testify how one person of character can truly change the world.

The Purpose of This Book

If professionals have a difficult time dealing with disturbed people, what chance does a regular person have? Might there be ways that ordinary people might confront these troubled souls, head-off more difficult problems, and find more fulfilling relationships? The answer of this book is "yes." Because if you don't recognize troubled thinking and deal directly with it, you will never find happiness in your relationships. You've already started by asking how your relationship ended like it is. This book will give you ways that you can deal directly with the misguided thinking and destructive behavior of the disturbed characters in your life. It will give you practical ways you can assess their behavior and secure you best chance for your relationship. It can help you accomplish the necessary change that has to happen.

It takes character to change. Character matters. A stronger character will help you listen empathically, speak judiciously without judgement, and act decisively. It takes courage and support to call out a disturbed character's bad behavior. This book can help you develop your game plan and then to act assertively, so you can be equipped and empowered to make necessary changes within yourself and your relationships.

What's in This Book

The book begins with hope, which is essential in any relationship. Then we begin a discussion about some of the obstacles that you encounter with disturbed characters and how to evaluate the personality of the person with whom you are in relationship. If that person has a disturbed or underdeveloped character, there are specific things to watch out for and anticipate. The troubled people that you may love and/or live with have certain predilections and behaviors that must be factored into account before you plan to do anything. You might also have your behaviors you have to deal with on your way to acting on your beliefs. After you've come to the realization that something has to change and you are sufficiently prepared to act, you also have to have an idea what your success will look like, what you are aiming for, what counts as healthy behavior. You will find that acting assertively to change a disturbed person's behavior happens through healthy confrontation. And if the person promises to change, this book will show you how a person who contrite acts and how can you trust the person to tell you the truth. But if despite your best efforts, this question might still remain: Do I stay or should I go? The book concludes with game-changing tools. As a bonus, there is an appendix that contains some helpful definitions and distinctions.

None of us wants to be miserable in our relationships. We all long to experience happiness and fulfillment. But there is no magic bullet. You didn't end up here magically, and no amount of wishing will change anything. There are things you need to know and wisely consider when dealing with disturbed characters. The practical tools in this book will help.

Chapter One
There Is Hope

Will He Ever Change?

Not long ago, I received the following letter from Jane[2] in Texas:

> After reading your book, *In Sheep's Clothing*,
> I recognized myself as the kind of "neurotic"
> person you describe, and the man I'm dating
> as a disturbed character. Unfortunately, it
> wasn't until I started to know better that I
> realized something wasn't quite right. But, as I
> hadn't been in a similar situation before and
> with him being a very smart person, it was
> hard for me to see things clearly.
>
> Now after reading more on your website, I
> have finally understood what the source of
> trouble was. He was just irresponsible,
> narcissistic, and hedonistic— all expressions
> of his underdeveloped character. I was just
> wondering what the treatment is if any? I've
> read here that such people don't usually
> change. Is there any hope for these types of
> people? Is there any real chance for our
> relationship?

---

[2] All names and identifying information in this book are changed for
confidentiality.

Letters like this one and comments over the years from folks prompted me to write this book.

***

The situation with most disturbed characters is not hopeless.

***

People often ask me, "Is there hope?" In my book, *Character Disturbance*, I address what it takes to make changes in persons with disturbed character. Contrary to popular belief, the situation with most disturbed characters is not hopeless. What is hopeless and pointless is trying to relate to or intervene with such people through traditional techniques and methods.

Traditional methods focus on feelings, unresolved emotional conflicts, and most especially, things hidden from consciousness. Traditional methods also try to give a person insight, which they don't have or won't consider, into problems as the principal way of solving them. But disturbed characters are already aware of the bad things they do and the reasons they do them. They like the way they do things, even if others don't. And their *feelings* are not at the root of problems. Instead, their distorted way of *thinking* about things and their irresponsible habitual *behaviors* are the culprits. So, dealing with disturbed characters effectively requires a completely different strategy from traditional methods.

***

Disturbed characters are *aware* but don't *care*.
They *see* but *disagree*.

***

These people must be confronted about their attitudes, ways or thinking, and their behavior; but confronted in a way that is healthy for both the person who is doing the confrontation and the person being confronted. But don't get the wrong idea, it's not only men who can have disturbed characters. There are plenty of disturbed women too. Just like there are women who wonder if the man in their life can change, there are plenty of men who are wondering if there is hope for their relationship with the significant woman in their life. Just as the face of evil can be masculine, it can be feminine as well.

When Evil Wears a Feminine Face

When we think of troubled people and particularly psychopaths, we tend to think of men — we find it hard to imagine these character traits in a woman—but women can be just as devoid of conscience as their male counterparts.

You may remember the trial of Jodie Arias in Phoenix, Arizona. She was accused of the brutal murder of her one-time boyfriend. Many of the actions, statements, and tactics of the defendant, bear striking similarity to those of another woman, Casey Anthony. In 2011 Casey was tried and acquitted of the murder of her two-year-old daughter. Whether or not Jodie Arias or Casey Anthony committed any crime, these trials provide a fascinating, albeit disquieting, glimpse into the possibility of evil when it wears a feminine face.

Psychopathy is the most extreme form of character disturbance and is defined primarily by the incapacity for empathy. Therefore psychopaths are unable to form a mature moral conscience as is well attested in the literature on the subject. But almost all of the examples of psychopathic characters referenced in the articles have been men. Similarly, almost all the research done on this pathology has been done on males. Even the instruments designed to assess the presence of psychopathic risk factors have been designed for use with males. While one can certainly make the argument that males make up a disproportionate percentage of these deeply impaired characters, perhaps a larger issue is that as a society, as badly as it might unnerve us to think that there are heartless predators among us, it doesn't seem to surprise us when these notorious characters turn out to be men. As a culture, we have a hard time believing that females of this very same character type exist. But after many years of working with the most severely disturbed characters among us, I can assure you that character disturbance respects no gender boundaries.

Some of the most chillingly conscience-devoid individuals I've come across over the years have been female. Still, while female psychopaths are identical in every respect to their male counterparts except, of course, for their gender, it's always amazed me how hesitant people are to accept the notion that females can also be so severely character disturbed. It seems that when it comes to recognizing evil, our vision and judgment can get clouded by a person's gender. The fact that we think of psychopaths as men and have designed our tests and treatment for men, says a lot more about us than about these individuals. Like the Anthony case, Arias's lawyer proposed a scenario designed to introduce doubt into the minds of the jurors as to whether her act was one of premeditated, cold-blooded murder. And because she was on trial for her life, even the slightest seed of doubt planted in the minds of the jurors could alter the jury's verdict and spell the difference between execution and life in prison.

One of the key qualities of psychopathic individuals is their penchant for and skill in lying. Lying for psychopaths is not just ordinary lying, but truly pathological lying—lying for its own sake, even when the truth would do just fine. And what sets psychopaths apart from other disturbed characters is the manner in which they lie. They lie without hesitation or compunction and without any apparent apprehension. You literally can't believe a word they say, because you never know when something coming out of their mouths is part of an elaborate "con." Still, remarkably, people listen to these characters. And in that listening, a degree of victimization occurs to the listener as the psychopath displays a calm coolness that in itself ought to be frightening.

For many of us, it seems unthinkable that a woman psychopath could have a glib, overly self-confident, haughty manner of someone like the serial killer Ted Bundy. I am not saying that male psychopaths can't present a deceptively charming and likable façade; but for our culture, there is something more unsettling in the poise that a psychopathic woman can display, perhaps because we have a hard time seeing it as sinister.

Those of us with consciences and empathy are a different lot. It's not that "people like us" can't do evil things; but like most Americans, we always want to think that somewhere inside everyone is something of worth and redeeming value. But again, our "natural" assumption that people are basically good might say more about us —our backgrounds and our experiences with family and friends.

Recently I had a friend in the hospital. Because I visited him so often, I became well acquainted with one of the nurses on the night shift. It wasn't long before we started talking about our philosophies of life. While we talked, I mentioned how I thought, and most people thought, that people were basically good. We all have that divine spark in us somewhere. The nurse, however, seriously disagreed. She said that in her experience, growing up how she did, she had a hard time believing that people were basically good. Her experience told her that people were essentially bad. But she thought she might know why I thought otherwise; she suspected that my background was probably similar to her husband's. Her husband grew up in a lovely middle-class home. He always had plenty, if not too much, to eat. He was loved and protected by both his parents, and he never had to worry about gunshots breaking his bedroom window. Even today, he believed in his core, that people, if given the chance, will do the right thing. Her growing up was different. In her household, food was hit or miss. Her mother—she never knew her dad— brought home all kinds of men. And even when she was pre-school age, she knew that she best beware of them. It wasn't uncommon for her to hear gunshots or have fighting wake her up in the middle of the night. She couldn't remember not being afraid. To her, people were always out to get you, and not in a good way. People were basically bad no matter how many chances you gave them.

After she told her story, I asked her why she was a nurse. "That," she answered, "is a complicated story, but suffice it to say that I'm afraid that I'm basically bad too. I'm just trying to be different. And I guess I believe in hope. That's what got me through and to where I am today."

Interestingly, given this woman's experience and the world view she developed, some previous psychological theories would have predicted that she would have actually become bad and behaved badly instead of fearing herself to be bad and doing her best to be good.

It causes us extreme dissonance to think that there people among us who have no conscience whatsoever. And although in recent years, psychologists have come to a general acceptance of the fact, especially when it comes to psychopathic men. But when evil wears a feminine face, we still can't allow ourselves to believe the worst.

The Cruelty of a Rescue

Before we launch into a discussion about dealing with the disturbed characters in our lives, I need to give you three foundational principles. If you follow these principles, you will be in a strategic position to be hopeful. First, there is hope because we want to help those we care about, but it is crucial to distinguish between helping and rescuing. Dealing with disturbed characters, even confrontation, is about help not about rescue. Whether parent, relationship partner, or therapist, we are often drawn into misguided attempts to rescue. We want to "take care of" rather than "care for." My attention was first drawn to this distinction by one of my professors. He cautioned us to beware of those people who wanted to "take care" of us. "That's a recipe for disaster in a therapeutic relationship, and it's no better for any personal relationship of significance."

A rush to rescue can, and probably will, prevent dysfunctional characters from recovering or finding health for themselves. One of the most important things I learned early on in my clinical work was the difference between genuine "help" and a "rescue." Help is what caring, principled people want to provide to those who have fallen victim to tragic circumstances not of their own making and from which they cannot reasonably recover on their own. Rescue is an unwarranted, undeserved, and often uninvited attempt to save someone from themselves.

You may be familiar with this story, but it illustrates the difference between rescue and helping. A teenager fell out of the family sailboat and for some reason, she wasn't wearing her life preserver. The water was deep and she couldn't swim to shore because of the strong tide. To her utter relief, a lifeguard appeared next to her; but every time she tried to grab onto him, he pushed her away. Again and again she lunged toward him, but each time he evaded her. Now, she was in a panic and she tried desperately to reach him. It wasn't long before her strength gave out. She decided that she was going to drown and the stupid lifeguard was happy to watch. The moment she gave up, the lifeguard took hold of her. Within minutes, he had her on the shore.

She was exhausted, but her fury shot more adrenaline through her veins. "You were going to let me drown. What's wrong with you?" The lifeguard just looked at her with sympathy. "The first thing a lifeguard learns is not to let the person grab them. If I had succumbed to that temptation, we both would have drowned. Get it? If you grab me, we both drown. If I grab you, we both live. Think about it. I can only help you if you surrender and let me do my job." We call what lifeguards do "rescue." And rescue is unwarranted, undeserved, and often an uninvited attempt to save someone from themselves. But if the lifeguard really cares for her, he'll also tell her to wear her life jacket next time. He'll *help* her avoid there being a "next time." By reminding her to wear a life jacket, he does what caring, principled people want to provide to those who have fallen victim to tragic circumstances not of their own making and from which they cannot reasonably recover on their own.

But our day-to-day relationships are a different matter, because here, inevitably, a rescuer is also an "enabler." An enabler doesn't offer real help. And in my experience, despite how well-intended this kind of rescuer might be, there's almost nothing crueler than a rescue. And while there are life-threatening emergencies when people need to be rescued, most times enabling someone allows them to continue self-destructive patterns of behavior.

***

Even if inadvertent, enabling someone is an act of cruelty.

***

Sometimes, those of us attracted to the helping professions have a bit too much of the natural "rescuer" in them. Helping professionals are often plagued by the need to be needed and the need to rescue others. Or we may believe that we are the only ones who can save this patient. And if we don't reckon honestly with these aspects of our personality, we're likely to have to learn some hard lessons when we begin practicing therapy. Here's a joke that I've actually heard several times at various professional conferences. The way one of my social worker friends tells it: two social workers are walking down a street in New York City on their way to a social workers' convention when a purse-snatcher on a bicycle breezes past, grabbing their purses. They give chase on foot, all the while shouting: "Stop that man! Stop him!!…. He's clearly in need of our help!"

Of course, mental health professionals aren't the only ones who can be rescuers/enablers. Parents are notorious for doing this with their children. The reasons are many, but mostly they center on the deep fear a parent has that something even more dreadful will happen to their wayward children if they don't do something to save them. Fear can be a powerful motivator. But it can also prevent a parent from standing ground and enforcing limits, when that's exactly what's needed to really help turn things around.

Partners in relationships can be rescuers/enablers too. There are even times when a person enters a relationship knowing the risks they face because of the obvious character impairments in their partner. Still, they entertain the notion that if they love their partner enough and nursemaid the wounds they suspect are at the root of their partner's dysfunction, they can save the day. But if the dysfunctional partner is skilled in the art of manipulation, the rescuing partner can be easily maneuvered into neglecting their own self-care on a repeated basis, even then it becomes evident that the character-impaired partner has only taken advantage of their tenderhearted nature.

But perhaps the cruelest part of a rescue has to do with giving the dysfunctional character just one more reason not to do the work they so sorely need to do to get better. Every valuable enterprise in life comes with a price tag of some sort. And the price tag for developing one's character is a lot of human sweat. But the benefits of that sweat are most often twofold: a better life and a better sense of self-efficacy and self-respect for triumphing over one's shortcomings.

The hard work of developing character yields a better life, sense of self-efficacy, and self-respect.

***

I'm not saying all of this from a purely intellectual or philosophical perspective or even out of sound clinical experience, although I can recount countless examples from my years of practice that would support what I'm saying. I can also speak from personal experience. I won't bore you with the details, but there was a time in my own life when things were quite a shipwreck. And unfortunately for me, those dysfunctional days persisted for a good while, because down deep I was confident my family and friends would come to my rescue. Then one day it happened. Those who loved me clearly saw the state of things; but for the first time, they let me be. I remember the exact moment when I sensed their emotional letting-go. I was shocked. And it was scary. It was sink or swim time. There was no one to prop me up or bail me out. It was also the moment my life changed forever. No, it didn't change miraculously or overnight. In fact, the ordeal I faced after the rescue rug was pulled out from under me was the most painful time I can remember. But it was worth every drop of sweat it took to turn things around. And, I know full well that things could have gone very differently. It's possible I couldn't have summoned the resources or the courage. I could have sunk, possibly even died. But I didn't. And I know that I wouldn't have had a chance at all at the life I enjoy today if I'd continued to be rescued. When I look back on it all, and on all the pain I caused myself and others — on all the pain it took to right things — nothing compares to the pain that most likely would have been invited into my life by another rescue.

Chasing after someone who's not asking for, emotionally ready for, or truly appreciative of genuine assistance in their bid to make things better for themselves and others is about the cruelest thing a person can do. Because hope will be found in the struggle.

Where there is struggle, there is hope.

Can We Save Our Loved Ones from Fatal Mistakes?

The second principle comes out of this question: Can we save those we love from making fatal mistakes? If rescue is unhealthy for a relationship, what can we do to prevent loved ones from making deadly errors? Is there hope for them? Over the years, I've gotten many inquiries about this particular issue. The inquiries have come from persons of both sexes of various ages and from several countries. Many times, the folks inquiring are already familiar with my writing (books and blogs) or they have made contact with me via email asking me to expand upon and/or clarify the principles I advocate in all my work. To summarize the gist of these inquiries, people ask: "How do I save someone I love from falling under the spell of a person I think is of bad or dangerous character, manipulative to be sure—possibly even a psychopath — who will likely abuse or hurt them in some way if something isn't done to prevent it?"

Most people asking this question are genuinely fearful and concerned, and not a few are desperate. They had already tried everything they know to help the person they cared about see the danger of becoming more involved, but to no avail. They ask because they see me as knowledgeable on the subject of character disturbance. They are hoping against all hope that I have a pearl of wisdom to offer that will enable them to rescue their loved one from the snares of disaster.

There's a mound of clinical research on the notion of "locus of control," which is an integral part of attribution theory. This term refers to where a person perceives that the power to influence or control events resides. A person who perceives the locus or point of control to be external might, for example, attribute the cause of events to happenstance or good or bad luck, whereas a person who perceives the locus of control to be internal will more likely attribute the cause of events to some action he or she took. And while it's generally healthy for a person to believe that they're not simply at the mercy of their external world, it's also potentially problematic to believe you have more power than you actually have to influence events. So I'm cautious when I advise people about just how much power they might actually have to influence the behavior of a loved one whom they perceive as perhaps making a fatal mistake about a relationship.

There's little doubt that we have the power to influence. For one thing, we can model or exemplify the kind of behavior we'd like to see someone else display. We can also encourage and reinforce behavior we see as desirable, as well as discourage or negatively consequent undesirable behavior. And we have the power to impart information, which is likely to be better received when our message is couched with obvious care and concern and delivered in a palatable manner. Of course, we can also use tactics to covertly coerce folks to do as we wish. But ultimately we must accept the fact that every individual holds the real control over their behavior.

***

Ultimately we must accept the fact that individuals hold the real control over their own behavior.

***

While we may have the power of choice and action, we do not have power over outcomes. There are too many cases of unintended consequences and Murphy's Law—the adage that says "Anything that can do wrong, will go wrong." We may delude ourselves into thinking that we can control "what happens next" but we can't. This is a really important concept to get your arms around when you are working to empower yourself. You have to be willing to let go of outcomes—even the anticipation of outcomes. The real power is in taking action, and while the outcome is not in your hands, it can be instructive and help you make course corrections to your plans. When we invest too much of our time, energy, and emotional passion into an enterprise over which we don't really have control, we end up fighting a lost cause and inviting feelings of helplessness, hopelessness, and eventually depression. We rob ourselves of hope.

Naturally, it's quite painful to watch helplessly while someone you love succumbs to the charm of a manipulator or invests in a relationship you fear is destined to be abusive or otherwise cause heartache. And it's also understandable to want to do everything in your power to stop it. But realizing where you ultimately do and don't have power is really the key, not only to personal peace of mind but also to a sense of self-efficacy.

When it comes to locus of control, it's important to get the balance right. When we fear that someone we care about is making a tragic mistake, we can honestly share our feelings, express our concern, encourage them to do otherwise, lend our support, model right action, and provide helpful information. Beyond that, we have little power. And we can certainly be there for that loved one if they simply have to learn a very hard lesson and later need a place of refuge or a shoulder to cry on. But we have to accept the fact that we can never truly save someone who isn't in a mental or emotional place to be rescued. But we can save ourselves a lot of grief and the sense of a loss of power when we accept the limits of our influence. So my answer to the question of whether we can save a loved one from making a fatal mistake is always the same: "No, we don't have that kind of ability, but we can save ourselves pain and depression, and we can probably do a lot more to help the person we care about when we are at peace with doing what we really can to influence them, while accepting the limits of our power."

Find Hope in Listening

The third principle is listen—first to your own best thinking and then to the other person. We might find that when we have time and space, or when we meditate, go for walks, or write down what we are feeling—whatever it is we do—we end up just listening to our thoughts, which behave like the loudest guests at the party. We might never hear from that quiet girl in the corner who looks really interesting. But when we can focus, we have the best chance to hear what is being said either in our own head or while sitting across the table from a partner.

Listening is the basic skill needed for therapists and counselors, but, even for us, listening to yourself has to come first. How do you to do it? Making time and space might not necessarily be enough. Listening is a whole body process. If we are listening in to the fluctuations of our energy levels, anxiety levels, muscle tension, to the speed and intensity of our breathing, the tone of our voice, any aches and pains we have, as living and changing processes (not just "I have a headache" or "I'm having a bad day"), then our thoughts will not get a chance to dominate the whole proceedings. They will take their own specific place, along with all the other feelings and intuitions, which make up our experience of the world.

Listening to ourselves is not just listening to our thoughts! When we tune in to everything we are aware of, not only do new understandings come, but often there is a sense of relief, gratefulness, and physical relaxation. When we are in this state it is so much easier to find creative, hopeful solutions.

Beware: Hearing Only What You Want to Hear

While it is vital to listen, we must also be aware that sometimes we hear only what we want to hear. And while we may all occasionally do this, manipulative people are experts at tuning-out, or as it's sometimes said, zoning-out. Disturbed people can also use your desire to listen as a way to blame and shame you, as well as play the victim—your victim.

Another behavior that disturbed characters frequently display is "selective attention" or "selective listening." Disturbed characters are good at seeing only what they want to see and hearing only what they want to hear. Stanton Samenow referred to this as "mental filtering" or "paying attention only to what suits him." And while we all can be prone to hearing only what we want, for disturbed people it is a principal way they resist internalizing the values, standards, and controls society wants them to adopt. One cannot be open to the idea of accepting a principle while simultaneously refusing to pay attention to it. One cannot empathize with another's concerns and tune out the other person at the same time. In short, one cannot be in the receptive/submissive mode and the combative/closed mode at the same time.

The tactic of selective attention goes hand in hand with the inattentive thinking patterns. When you start to discuss a problem behavior with a disordered character, they almost always know what you're about to say before you actually say it. And, they almost immediately start tuning you out. The reason they don't want to hear it is that they are not prepared to submit themselves to the principle of conduct you and they both know underlies the confrontation you are about to make. So, when they start tuning you out, you have absolute assurance they have no intention of changing course.

Many times, selective attention is mistaken for an attention deficiency, especially in children and adolescents. Some young persons, through no fault of their own, have trouble sustaining focus and attention. They might be able to do so when hyper-stimulated, but otherwise they have problems attending to a task. Selective attention is different, although it can accompany an attention deficiency. Many parents intuitively know that their child's hearing improves instantly when they're talking about something they know the child wants or likes.

To counteract selective hearing selectively speak. One of the ways I confirm whether or not someone is tuning me out deliberately and to test whether they were in the slightest ready to receive counsel is simply not to talk to them unless they at least appeared attentive and receptive. This is, by far, one of my most powerful therapeutic techniques and one of the most empowering tools for persons in relationships with individuals of disturbed character.

Take Away

If you wonder how your relationship has ended up where it is, or if you wonder if your partner can change, there is hope. There is hope for most relationships even with many disturbed characters, but be aware that your best course is often to refrain from rescue. Help and rescue are different. Help is what caring, principled people want to provide to those who have fallen victim to tragic circumstances not of their own making and from which they cannot reasonably recover on their own. Rescue is an unwarranted, undeserved, and often uninvited attempt to save someone from themselves.

You can't save people from making fatal mistakes, but there is hope. When we fear that someone we care about is making a tragic mistake, we can honestly share our feelings, express our concern, encourage them to do otherwise, lend our support, model right action, and provide helpful information. Beyond that, we have little power. And we can certainly be there for that loved one if they simply have to learn a very hard lesson and later need a place of refuge or a shoulder to cry on.

Focus and listen. When we focus and listen, we have the best chance to hear what is being said in our own head and what the person across the table is saying. When we tune in to everything we are aware of, not only do new understandings come, often there is a sense of relief, gratefulness, and physical relaxation. When we are in this state, it is so much easier to find creative, hopeful solutions.

Be prepared that disturbed people will use your willingness to listen against you and as a way to manipulate you. They are especially good at selective attention. Your best counter is selective talking.

Empowerment Tools

1. There is hope because we want to help those we care about, but it is crucial to distinguish between helping and rescuing. Dealing with disturbed characters is about help not about rescue.

2. We cannot save those we love from making fatal mistakes.

3. Listen to your own best thinking and open yourself to listen to the other person. But know that there will be things you don't want to hear.

4. Use selective talking when the other person tunes you out.

Chapter Two
Loving and Living in a Character-Disturbed World

The Unreasonable Thinking of Disturbed Characters

It will come as no surprise to those of you who love and live with disturbed characters that they have no sense of balance, fairness, or compromise. The unreasonable demands they inflict make their behavior a conundrum to other people and a frequent source of conflict and relationship distress.

Disordered characters are unrealistic in their thinking about life and the world around them. They also tend to harbor excessive expectations. This is not to say that we are talking about people who "think big" or those who see possibilities where others don't. The difference between creative people and disturbed people is the expectations of disturbed people are one-sided, and they tend to set unattainable standards for everyone else, while feeling no concomitant sense of obligation to meet the expectations of others.

***

Disturbed people set unattainable standards for everyone and feel no obligation to meet those same expectations.

***

Disturbed characters expect too much from their government, from their bosses, their spouses, and children—anyone who has any kind of relationship with them. And their expectations are most always unreasonable. They expect others to trust them, even before they've done anything that proves that they truly deserve any trust. They expect others to be attentive to their wants and needs and to cater to their whims. They expect things to go their way—all the time. They expect a lot from everyone, usually putting considerable stress on a relationship.

If disordered characters expected themselves to measure up to the same standards they set for everyone else, they wouldn't be nearly as difficult to live with or work with. What's more, if they imposed the kinds of standards on themselves that they try to impose on others, they wouldn't engage in so many of the antisocial and other problem behaviors they so frequently display.

Because disturbed characters have no sense of balance, fairness, or compromise, their thinking over time eventually leads to develop a rigidly demanding attitude. The demands they bring to a relationship are a source of conflict and distress. A partner might try to reason with them to no avail. Their thinking is too focused on their own expectations of others to be refocused on what they might do differently to get their wants and needs met.

***

A rigidly demanding attitude brings conflict and distress.

***

Therapeutic interventions with disordered characters can be a real challenge, especially when inordinate expectations are placed on the counselor. Many counselors are intimidated by the subtle challenge to their capabilities that such a stance presents. Others, especially those who see their role as one of "helper," can unconsciously feel obligated to try and meet unreasonable demands. In my work, one thing I have learned is the importance of being clear, from the earliest moments of the therapeutic encounter that the burden for change rests squarely on the disordered character. All the expectations are on him. I also know that I'll have to confront his unreasonable thinking many times during the course of treatment. But each time I encounter it, I'm careful to confront it directly and put the burden for change back squarely where it belongs.

Understanding Aggression

To deal with the rigid demands of disordered characters, traditional psychology has overly focused on, and perhaps been obsessed with, their fears and anxieties. Classical psychology paradigms even sought to define people's personalities by the ways they "run" from things they unconsciously feared or the ways they "defend" themselves against perceived threats from the outside world and from the experience of anxiety. In short, classical psychology viewed people mainly as runners and largely unwitting runners at that. And the classical paradigms viewed all the psychological problems we can have as stemming from the unhealthy or inadequate ways we avoid or defend ourselves from the things we fear. As a result, classical psychology failed us all in explaining a large segment of human behavior.

I've long made the point that most of us do an infinitely greater amount of fighting than we do running in our daily lives. By fighting I do not mean being physically violent. Physical violence is just one of many forms of human aggression. And it's by no means the predominant form. While human beings do fight, most of it is done in various nonviolent ways. We don't fight, as many have assumed, only when we feel threatened or afraid, we also fight merely because we want our own way. And not all fighting we do is bad either. Sometimes it's both appropriate and necessary to fight, for example when we fight in line with our principles for the things we truly need and with the constraint and discipline necessary to respect the rights, needs, and boundaries of others. In this case fighting might even the healthiest thing we can do. That's largely what assertive behavior is all about, and healthy confrontation falls into this category. But clearly, some kinds of fighting are particularly problematic, as is especially the case with the subtle, underhanded, unprincipled fighting, which is what I call covert-aggression, which I address below, because it is almost always involved in interpersonal manipulation.

There's been a lot of misunderstanding about the nature of human aggression, and this misunderstanding contributes to our dis-ease about confrontation. But much of this misunderstanding is also due to the rampant misuse of important psychological terms, such as aggression, even by mental health professionals. Aggression is the forceful energy we all expend to survive and prosper, and it usually involves attempting to secure a desired goal, to remove obstacles in the way of achieving those goals, or to remove perceived threats to our well-being. Our language reflects our deep-seated awareness of the true nature of aggression when we say things like: "If you want something, you have to fight for it" or when we encourage those who are sick or infirm to rally their resources and "battle" their cancers, infections, or other diseases. Humans have always done a lot of fighting. It's a part of life. When we're not making some kind of love, we're generally waging some kind of war.

***

Aggression is not synonymous with violence.

***

How we fight is another matter. It's also of paramount importance to realize that aggression is not synonymous with violence. Here is an example of the kind of aggression I'm talking about. Perhaps you've been cut off or driven with an aggressive driver who dodges and weaves through traffic just to shave off that extra second he knows he needs to have. He expects everyone to get out of his way. And heedless of the consequences of his reckless behavior, he keeps going. This person is not driven by fear or insecurity, but by his desire to plow over, or perhaps obliterate, any obstacles.

The following is a basic summary of a framework that can help conceptualize the various subtypes of human aggression. Given that aggression is central to who we are as human beings, let's review some of its many forms and distinctions. Some of these types of aggression are especially problematic, so I will discuss those at length below.

1. Reactive aggression: a person aggresses, usually in a defensive posture, in response to a threat to his/her safety or security.

2. Predatory aggression: a person aggresses for the pure purpose of victimization.

3. Covert aggression: the aggressor attempts to conceal aggressive behavior and nefarious intent to increase the odds of gaining advantage over a target. This is often confused with passive-aggression.

4. Overt aggression: the aggressor openly and unabashedly lashes out against a target.

5. Direct aggression: the aggressor directly attacks a target Indirect aggression: the aggressor employs some type of intermediary entity or action to attack a target.

6. Active aggression: the aggressor does something actively to injure/exploit/gain advantage over a target.

7. Passive aggression: the aggressor fails to do, resists doing, or refuses to do something as a way of frustrating a target.

Reactive Aggression

Aggression can be purely reactive. That is, it can be a response to a sudden, unexpected threat to well-being. Reactive aggression has certain characteristics, and it's long been assumed that all aggression is prompted only by fear and in response to a perceived threat. An illustration of these characteristics would be a cat sitting on a front porch who sees the neighborhood pit bull rounding the corner. It does certain characteristic things. It arches its back. Its hair stands on end. It brandishes its claws. It hisses. It signals a willingness to fight if it must. But it doesn't really want to fight. It's primarily afraid and more than anything it wants the threat to go away. If the pit bull goes its merry way without approaching the cat, the episode is over. The cat will not aggress. Reactive aggression is spontaneous, rooted in fear, and "defensive" in character, and the goal is the avoidance of victimization.

Predatory Aggression

Other aggressive personalities include the unbridled-aggressive, who is frequently in conflict with the law; the channeled-aggressive, who generally limits ruthlessness to non-criminal activity; the covert-aggressive, who cloaks their cruelty under a veneer of civility and manipulates others in the process; and the sadistic aggressive, whose principal aim is to demean and injure others. But by far the most pathological aggressive personality is the one I prefer to label the predatory-aggressive personality. All of the aggressive personalities are among the most seriously disturbed in character of the various personality types, and the predatory-aggressive personality is the most seriously character disordered.

Predatory-aggressive personalities (i.e., psychopaths or sociopaths), also known by some researchers as "instrumental," consider themselves superior to the rest of the human race. They view individuals with inhibitions rooted in emotional bonding to others as inferior creatures and, therefore, their rightful prey. When a cat spies a mouse in the corner of a room that it fancies for a meal, it doesn't make noise (hiss) or arch its back. It keeps its claws retracted and stays low to the ground so as to maintain quiet and low visibility. In fact, it does nothing to signal aggression but attempts to conceal it until the moment of attack. Its aggression is not prompted by fear of the mouse but rather desire for the mouse. And it's not prompted by anger, either (an extremely important thing for folks to remember when making presumptions about the connection between anger and aggression — the basis for most so-called anger management paradigms). Predatory or instrumental aggression is rooted purely in desire, is strictly offensive in character, and the goal is victimization.

Many labels have been given to the personality type I call the predatory-aggressive. The term psychopath was used in the early twentieth century but was later more commonly replaced with the term sociopath. However, recently, the term psychopath has regained popularity. But because I think personality is best define by an individual's "style" of relating to others, I think the term predatory most accurately describes the interpersonal *modus operandi* of these individuals.

Through the years, several opinions have been offered about what lies at the core of this most serious personality disturbance. Hervey Cleckley in his landmark book, *The Mask of Sanity: An Attempt to Clarify Some Issues about the So-Called Psychopathic Personality* noted that their extraordinary difference in makeup from most people, especially with respect to matters of conscience or qualities long thought to comprise the "soul" of humanity bordered on an almost psychotic level of difference. Robert D. Hare in his popular book, *Without Conscience: The Disturbing World of the Psychopaths Among Us* and many scholarly articles, points out that their lack of capacity to feel emotionally connected to or bonded with the rest of humanity is at the root of their "callous, senseless, and remorseless use and abuse of others."

These individuals are radically different creatures from most human beings. Denial of this reality has been the undoing of many who are later victimized. But in my opinion, at the root of their pathology is not so much their different wiring, but their extraordinarily positive appraisal of their difference from the rest of us. In a most malevolent example of malignant narcissism to the extreme, these individuals consider themselves beings superior to the rest of the human race. They view individuals with inhibitions rooted in emotional bonding to others as inferior creatures and, therefore, their rightful prey. This is the justification they use for their pattern of predatory engagement with others.

If it weren't bad enough that some individuals are in neurotic denial about the uniquely abnormal makeup of predatory aggressive personalities, many are also easily taken in by their manipulative skill. Predatory aggressors know human nature perhaps better than anyone. Most have made a study of it. They know every human vulnerability, shortcoming, yearning, need, and wish. And they know how to mimic just about everything that is human, from emotion to empathy. But it's all part of the unrelenting con game of taking advantage of those perceived to be at heart an inferior species.

I recently answered an inquiry from a man who wondered if his therapist had advised him correctly that psychopaths are "unable" to tell right from wrong, in much the same way as someone who suffers from an active psychosis. I responded to him that these individuals understand quite well what other people consider to be necessary standards for civil human relations. They could, if they chose, conform their conduct to such standards. However, they see these standards as just another example of a deficient species restraining itself from self-advancement. And, because they consider it a mark of their superiority not to be encumbered by such concerns, they choose not to abide by any law other than the law of personal gain.

While it might appear that there are many similarities between manipulative people and those generally referred to as psychopaths, not all aggressive personalities are as devoid of conscience and as disturbed in character as the predatory-aggressive personality, despite the fact that these individuals have generally refined their manipulative skill to nearly an art form. The reason, however, that such personalities are so successful in their predation is more insidious.

The fact is that humanistic-leaning counselors and positive-minded people in general find it hard, if not impossible, to believe that there are predators among us who are so cold-heartedly dangerous. It's not so much because of what dire circumstances life might have meted out to the predator, but rather because of how differently they are wired as organisms. In the end, that's what enables positive-minded people to be victimized by the predators they encounter. They don't trust their gut feelings in the presence of the predator and allow themselves to be duped by their tactics, believing all the while that their victimizer simply couldn't be as callously, senselessly, heartlessly, and remorselessly abusive and exploitative (and most especially, as unlike themselves) as their intuition suspected.

Covert Aggression

Aggression can also be covert. That is, it can be carefully cloaked so that aggressive intent is concealed from open observation. Covert aggression is at the heart of much interpersonal manipulation and emotional abuse. People often get conned and abused by others, because they fail to spot their aggressive intentions and behaviors until after they've already been victimized. But covert aggression is a particularly insidious type of fighting. That's because victims can have a lot of understandable difficulty recognizing it in the first place and then defending themselves once they sense it. Being the victim of covert aggression can make you feel crazy. In your gut, you think someone's trying to get the better of you or abuse you in some way, but you can't point to anything clear and obvious to back up your hunch. It's a like getting whiplash. You don't really realize what's happened to you until after damage has already been done. Even once you get an idea of what's going on, it's hard to respond well. The covert aggressor has usually succeeded at throwing you on the defensive, and when you're in such a state, it's hard to think clearly about how you might better handle yourself.

Covert-aggressive personalities are the archetypal wolves in sheep's clothing. These individuals are not openly aggressive in their interpersonal style. In fact, they do their best to keep their aggressive intentions and behaviors carefully masked. They can often appear quite charming and amiable, but underneath their civil façade, they are just as ruthless as any other aggressive personality. They are devious, underhanded, and subtle in the ways they abuse and exploit others. They have usually amassed an arsenal of interpersonal maneuvers and tactics that have enabled them to effectively manipulate and control those in relationships with them. The covert-aggressive personality employs a potent one-two punch: the covert-aggressive conceals aggressive intent to ensure you never really see what's coming; and he or she exploits your normal sensitivities, conscientiousness and other vulnerabilities to manipulate you into succumbing.

The tactics they use are effective because they accomplish two objectives very effectively at the same time:

1. The tactics conceal obvious aggressive intent. When the covert-aggressive is using the tactics, the other person has little objective reason to suspect that he is simply attempting to gain advantage over them.

2. The tactics covert-aggressive personalities use effectively play on the sensitivity, conscientiousness, and other vulnerabilities of most persons—especially neurotic individuals—and therefore effectively quash any resistance another person might have to give-in to the demands of the aggressor.

This one-two punch—never really seeing what's coming and being vulnerable to succumbing to them—is at the heart of why most people get manipulated. For example, a wife confronts her husband about not spending as much time as she wants him to spend with the family. He might retort that he constantly feels as if unreasonable demands are being placed on him by her (casting himself as the victim); that he works hard to provide for his family but no one seems to appreciate it (casting himself as the suffering, under-valued servant); and that she never has anything good to say about him and is always complaining (using the techniques of shaming and guilt-tripping). Within moments, the woman's good intention to correct a problem in family relationships is now framed as a heartless attack on an unappreciated devoted husband and father. If the wife buys into the tactics, she will be successfully manipulated. She won't see the situation as one in which she is in a relationship with a person who puts his own desires first and his family's a distant second. In fact, she might not view him as an aggressor at all and may even come to believe that she is the unjust attacker. She'll probably relent and remain under her partner's dominance and control.

As you can see from the preceding example, aggressive personalities that use such tactics to bring potential adversaries to submission are anything but passive in their interpersonal styles. Yet for years many have erroneously applied the label "passive-aggressive" to such behaviors. Furthermore, personalities such as the husband described in the example above are very different from the kind of personalities that are appropriately labeled passive-aggressive personalities.

When people use the terms "passive-aggressive" or "passive aggression" what they really mean is "covert aggression." I usually hear the term "passive-aggressive" used incorrectly to describe the subtle, hard to detect, but yet deliberate, calculating and underhanded tactics that manipulators and other disturbed characters use to intimidate, control, deceive, and abuse others. That's what covert aggression is all about. Although this kind of aggression is often subtle or concealed, there's absolutely nothing "passive" about it. It's very active, albeit veiled, aggression.

Covert-aggressive personalities are very different from passive-aggressive personalities, because these covert aggressors are anything but passive. They are actively aggressive personalities who know how to keep their aggressive agendas carefully cloaked. Dealing with them is like getting whiplash. You don't know how badly you've been taken advantage of until long after the damage is done. They are, perhaps, the most manipulative of all personalities with the possible exception of the psychopathic.

Passive Aggression

Passive aggression is a relatively healthy form of aggression. Passive aggression is, as its name suggests, aggression through passivity as opposed to any type of "active" aggression (aggressing by what you do and don't do). It's not answering your mate when you're mad at him and don't particularly want to talk to him. It's not returning a phone call when you don't really want to connect with the other person in the first place. But it is "forgetting" once again to pick up the dry cleaning that the partner you're mad at asked you to pick up. Passive aggression can be a powerful and frustrating strategy when carried to extremes.

When Gandhi's followers simply stood fast and would not move out of the army's line of fire, although many perished, their "passive resistance" eventually brought an occupying empire to its knees. Most of the time, however, passive aggression is a relatively self-defeating strategy, especially when it comes to getting what you need in a relationship.

The eminent researcher Theodore Millon, in *Personality Disorders in Modern Life* by Theodore Million, Carrie M. Millon, Sarah Meagher, Seth Grossman, and Rowena Ramnath, (p. 472), describes passive-aggressive personalities as having an "active-ambivalent" pattern of relating to others. That is, they are ambivalent about whether to adhere primarily to a staunchly independent mode of conduct or to rely primarily on others to tend to their emotional needs. As a result, they engage in a continuous pattern of vacillation between the two extremes. Ask them where they want to go for dinner and they will tell you to decide. Pick a place and they will complain that they don't really like it that well and don't want to go there. Invite them to pick a place of their own liking and they will complain that they asked you to decide. Tell them of another preference and they will be lukewarm to your suggestion. It goes on and on. Therapists who treat passive-aggressive personalities know this kind of scenario well. Their client will pelt them with pleas for assistance. But when the therapist recommends a course of action, the client will come up with ten reasons why he or she can't do what the therapist prescribes. When the therapist throws up his or her hands in exasperation, the client will wail and complain that nobody cares. It's a horribly self-defeating vicious circle of ambivalence.

Passive-aggressive personality types have the misfortune to be "stuck" on the proverbial fence of emotional development. In their heart of hearts, they want to be emotionally independent, answer to no one, and chart their own course. But they have deep doubts about their ability to do so. And because they're so sensitive to shame, they never want to risk doing anything that invites the possibility of failure. So, they end up chronically seeking the support of others. Still, they detest having to rely on others and especially resent the notion of caving in to others demands or expectations. So when it comes to functioning emotionally on a primarily independent vs. dependent or autonomous vs. self-doubting plane, they are deeply divided, and that's what causes all the problems. They want to do things their way; but in their hesitancy, they look for direction from others. When someone gives that direction, they resent it and then resist complying. It's their penchant for that frequent passive-resistance (i.e., passive aggression) that makes living with them so frustrating.

For example, there was a couple who'd been married for about nine years. Neither liked to cook, so they would eat out quite frequently. Almost every discussion about where to eat ended up in a fight. Marge, who was hesitant to assert herself, despite having lots of ideas about where she might like to go, would ask Fred where he wanted to go. Fred, being a solidly independent sort, always had a ready opinion to offer. Marge, hating to simply go along with everything Fred wanted (and also having some ideas of her own), would express some reservation. Fred, not wanting a fight to ensue, would indicate his willingness to let Marge make the call. But Marge, who didn't want to be blamed for picking a disappointing place, would again defer to Fred. Fred would make another call, and again, Marge would resist. This back and forth exchange would continue until Fred was ready to rip his hair out. Sometimes, he would lash out. Marge, on the other hand, would shut down and give Fred "the silent treatment." The next day, she might not so accidentally "forget" once again to pick up his shirts at the dry cleaners. On and on it went with this couple, day after day, deeply ensconced in the passive-aggressive "dance."

As those who've lived or worked with passive-aggressive personalities know, they can be whiney, stubborn, difficult, withholding, and very, very frustrating to deal with. Fortunately, getting them help in therapy is a much more hopeful proposition than getting help for the covert aggressors they're frequently mistaken for. Because they inwardly really want to be more autonomous and independent, but they are simply hung up in that pursuit primarily by their shame sensitivity. Helping them feel better about themselves by experiencing small successes in making more assertive choices is generally all it takes to eventually bring them out of their passive-aggressive pattern.

The passive-aggressive personality style is fundamentally self-defeating, so it's always empowering when a person who has these tendencies overcomes them with proper help. It's also a big relief for anyone who might have to live or work with them. Getting off the fence is what it takes. Once the person has decided to function in a more autonomous, independent way, and to make peace with episodic failure, their typical negativism gives way to greater joy and vitality, and living with them can be a much more harmonious enterprise.

What Disturbed Aggressive Personalities Hold in Common

Aggression, in and of itself, is not detrimental to character development, but there are disturbed aggressive personalities who possess characteristics common to narcissistic personalities. Indeed, there are some theorists who view aggressive personalities as merely aggressive variations of the narcissistic personality. But the principal distinguishing characteristic of these aggressive personalities is, not so much their narcissism, but their penchant for aggression. Aggressive personalities have more in common with one another than they have differences between them.

First, they actively seek the superior or dominant position in any relationship or encounter. There is a saying in the real estate business that there are three things that really matter: location, location, and…location. With aggressive personalities, there are three things that really matter regardless of the situation they're in: position, position, and…of course, position!

Second, they abhor submission to any entity that one might view or conceptualize as a "higher power" or authority. They are fundamentally at war with anything that stands in the way of their unrestrained pursuit of their desires. That often includes the rules, dictates, and expectations of society. Some will accede to or give assent to demands placed on them when it is expedient to do so, but in their heart of hearts, they never truly subordinate their wills.

Third, they are ruthlessly self-advancing, generally at the expense of others. They actively and deliberately seek to exploit and victimize others when to do so will further their own ends. Whereas the narcissist simply doesn't consider the rights or needs of others, the aggressive character tramples the rights and needs of others to satisfy their own desires.

Fourth, they have a pathological disdain for the truth. Aggressive characters don't just disregard the truth, they're actively at war with it. Truth is the great equalizer, and the aggressive personality always wants to maintain a position of advantage. So, they deliberately play very loose with the truth when they're not flat out lying to con or dupe you. They don't want you to "have their number." That upsets the balance of power.

Fifth, they lack internal "brakes." They don't stop themselves when they're on their mission. Like a rolling train with no means to stop, they exercise little control over their impulses.

Sixth, they view life as a combat stage, with every event in life having only four possible outcomes:

> I win, you lose.
> You win, I lose.
> I win, you win.
> I lose, you lose.

Their greatest desire is for the first possible outcome. They like it best when they win and you lose. For them, this is the clearest indication that they have emerged the victor in a contest and have secured the dominant position. Contrarily, they abhor the notion that you might win and they will lose. They will resist this potential outcome with every fiber in their body. Such an outcome puts them in the inferior or subordinate position, which they detest. Aggressive characters will reluctantly but not so graciously accept win-win outcomes. That is, they'll stop warring with you if they think they've achieved some sort of victory out of the encounter, even if you also get something you want. Tragically, if it becomes clear that they are most certainly headed for defeat, aggressive characters often won't go down easily. They often want to take someone else with them. It takes some of the sting out of defeat.

Take Away

Aggression can be undisciplined and destructive, but it can also be carefully tempered with concern for others and can be constructive in the amelioration of human misery. When people fight fairly and confront constructively for what they need, while being careful to respect the rights, needs, and boundaries of others, their behavior is best labeled assertive. But disturbed aggressive persons strive to win at all costs and make you lose at all costs. But assertive behavior when it results in healthy confrontation has power to bring change.

In the next chapter, we will take a closer look at the difference between assertive and aggressive behavior.

***

Healthy confrontation is assertive behavior and therein lies its power to bring change.

***

Disturbed aggressive personalities are fundamentally at war with anything that stands in the way of their unrestrained pursuit of their desires. They have no sense of balance, fairness, or compromise. The unreasonable demands they inflict on others are a frequent source of conflict and relationship distress. There are different types of aggression, each bringing its own style of relating to others. But how **we** fight, how **we** deal with conflict can be characterized by what we actively do versus what we refuse to do, and this difference in behavior is the heart of healthy confrontation.

Empowerment Tools

1. Be aware of patterns of behavior. Look for the one-two punch: not seeing what's coming and being vulnerable to succumbing to unreasonable demands that the disturbed person does not apply to themselves.

2. Nonviolent fighting can be a good thing if you are careful to respect the rights, needs, and boundaries of others.

3. You have a choice. Your feelings and beliefs may shape your thinking, but you have a choice about how you act as does the person you confront. If you don't or can't or if he or she doesn't or won't, seek professional guidance.

Chapter Three
When Something Has to Change: Be Assertive

Aha! The Power of Realization

It's not so much seeing as doing that usually creates the most powerful *Aha!* moments in our lives.

Recently I got an unusual email from a woman with whom I'd worked long ago on ways to improve her interpersonal skills. Nellie[3] is conscientious and always wants to get things right. But if you were to ask her friends and associates, they might tell you she also tends to be obsessive about things—so exacting, demanding, detail oriented, and mission focused, that she seems to forget she's working with other human beings who have feelings. This behavior has always made it hard for her to build intimate relationships and alliances. Nellie is an intelligent, insightful woman, who one day asked herself, "How did we end up here?" She fully understood, at an intellectual level, the things I discussed with her and advised her to do to improve her social skills. But it wasn't until she made a concerted effort to put some principles we'd talked about into practice that she had that proverbial *Aha!* moment that changed everything.

---

[3] In this book, all names and potentially identifying facts and circumstances are altered for purposes of anonymity and confidentiality.

Nellie told me she had been working intensively on a complicated project with one of her colleagues with whom relations had always been strained. Both were highly opinionated and would frequently clash, because each believed they were right and neither could find room to compromise or, at least, grant some credence to the other's point of view. It bothered each of them that they couldn't be closer, because each admired the other. Her co-worker found Nellie not only stubborn in her convictions but also prone to vindictive, hurtful behavior when she didn't get her way. I had once challenged Nellie about whether it was more important for her to be right or to be valued, appreciated, and have good relationships. I proposed to her that, with the exception of truly crucial circumstances, she might find room in her heart to set aside judgment and give ground on some of the smaller matters and to do so frequently as a way of building a relationship of mutual respect and trust. While she clearly understood the principle intellectually and gave verbal assent to it, she couldn't seem to bring herself to do it.

For the first time ever she found herself doing something differently. That sparked her *Aha!* moment. An important point here. The old notion in psychology has been that people first "see" then they change their ways. It rarely works that way. Rather, they behave differently first, experience the consequences, then "see" the errors of their former ways. And even after they've seen the light, their old habits continue to have power over them, so they sometimes do the same old dysfunctional things. Not only do people have to practice different behavior, they also need a lot of reinforcement for doing things differently. This was definitely true for Nellie.

A dispute had arisen between her and her co-worker about how best to present the most important part of their project to upper management. Instead of insisting she was right and that it had to be done her way, Nellie indicated to her co-worker that, because how they presented their project was a relatively minor consideration in the grand scheme of things and because she not only wanted her co-worker to feel supported and respected but also wanted to feel supported and respected by her, she would simply set aside what she believed to be her better judgment in this case and allow the outcome be their teacher. To her great surprise, something happened she never thought possible: her co-worker gave her a huge embrace, told her how much she'd always revered her and how much she had longed for a better relationship between them. On top of that, the co-worker quickly added how happy she would be to change course if it turned out that Nellie had been right all along. For Nellie, this was a seminal moment.

One of the many things I've learned from working within a cognitive-behavioral framework to help people change is how the best kinds of insight usually come about. It's one thing to muse intellectually about a concept, and it's quite another to really "get it" as an important life lesson by actually doing something differently and then experiencing the consequences. Truly powerful *Aha!* moments don't happen by merely reading something, hearing something, or imagining something but by actually doing something and witnessing the effects. Experience is our best teacher and the impression it leaves is almost always deeper. Of course, old habits die hard, which is why it's so important to give yourself both acknowledgment and reinforcement for doing things differently.

Maybe you've had an *Aha!* in your relationship. Or maybe you're in the midst of experiencing one now. You have surprised yourself by your own behavior and realized that something has changed. Perhaps that is why you bought this book. You know that something has changed and you are ready to take another step. You've had an experience that has led you to the conclusion that your relationship is not what it needs to be and you are looking for a way to put that experience to use.

However, some kinds of personalities don't seem to profit from their experiences, which is a hallmark of the nature of their character disturbance. You may be in a relationship with a person like this. But most of us can and do learn from trying new approaches, which is why it's so important for a cognitive-behaviorally oriented therapist to pay adequate attention to the behaviors most needing change and to provide the necessary encouragement for making those changes. And if you want to confront a disturbed person, it is also important for you to pay attention to the specific behavior that needs to be changed as well. But remember that for someone to behave differently, it's not in the understanding that they suddenly start doing things differently, but rather in the doing of things differently that they truly come to see the important realities of life.

***

It's not in the understanding that people start doing things differently, but it's in doing things differently.

***

Tools of Assertiveness: Decide, Plan, Act

Coming to an *Aha!* moment requires assertive behavior, which calls for the ability to address issues non-defensively and with objectivity. In business there is a solid consensus among management and strategists about the formula for success when dealing with a concern:

- **Identify.** Determine the exact nature of the presenting problem.

- **Decide.** Resolve to commit time, energy, and resources to addressing the problem.

- **Plan.** Define your goals, then devise short- and long-term objectives to reach those goals as well as the methods you need to employ to further your objectives.

- **Execute.** After you've planned your work, then work your plan.

- **Evaluate.** Assess both the reasonableness of your goals and objectives your as well as your progress on meeting those objectives and the effectiveness of your methods.

- **Modify.** Make necessary course corrections in your plan. Then resume working your plan.

- **Act.** Resume working your plan.

These guidelines for managerial assertiveness have proven their value in the competitive workplace many times over. But as a therapist providing assertiveness training to clients, I found three of the components outlined above to be of paramount importance. When it comes to asserting yourself and maximizing your chances for success, the rules are as simple as 1-2-3: decide, plan, then act.

***

**To foster an assertive personality,
actively taking care of yourself in a way that also
respects the rights and needs of others.**

***

I once counseled a young woman whose financial situation made it clear to her that she needed a different job. While she truly hated many aspects of her existing situation, especially her level of compensation. She was at the top of the pay scale for her position and there were no higher paying alternatives available within the organization. There was one thing, however, that kept her hooked—security. She had been with the company a long time, had decent working relationships with many of her co-workers, and knew both the company and her position within it to be stable and secure. So as badly as she needed to make a change, she was hesitant to take the inevitable risks associated with leaving what was already both familiar and safe. While she frequently insisted she had explored other opportunities, she always seemed to find some reason that other possibilities probably wouldn't work out. Eventually, it became clear. She really hadn't made the decision to leave; and until she did, she couldn't possibly commit to an alternate plan of action.

Making a decision to do something is often less of a rational thought process and more of an internal emotional reckoning. Naturally, it would have been unnecessarily reckless for this woman to simply turn in her resignation with no viable alternatives in sight. But all of her so-called exploring of other alternatives was half-hearted at best, because she hadn't yet really made the decision in her heart to leave the safety of her current job and accept the risks associated with change. So she was going nowhere fast. The decision she needed to make had more to do with coming to some inner peace about giving up the security she enjoyed in favor of the bigger career opportunity and the better compensation that she so sorely needed. Once she came to terms with the reasons for her ambivalence and actually made the firm decision to leave, everything changed. From that moment on, planning her next moves more naturally fell into place.

She was then able to fashion some short- and long-term goals. For the short-term, she would use some of her ample accumulated leave time to seriously interview at other companies. For the longer term, she would map out the pros and cons and costs and benefits of the viable placement alternatives she found, perhaps even being willing to accept a position at a less than perfect place for the intermediate term as a sort of stepping stone to a more ideal placement she sought for the long run. Once she was sure of the soundness of her plan, the only thing left was to put the plan into action, never looking back, only looking forward and making adjustments when necessary. She did work this plan and in the end, secured a great position at a stellar company with good pay and regular performance bonuses, and she quickly became part of the upper management team. But there's no way she could have gotten where she did without taking that first step of making the firm decision to make a change, then holding fast to the vision of where she wanted to be and faithfully working her plan to get there.

When we first began working together, I would never have described this woman as an assertive personality. In fact, she was much more like the ambivalent types I describe in *Character Disturbance* and *In Sheep's Clothing*. And her ambivalence extended far beyond the indecisiveness she displayed when first contemplating a change of jobs. She was ambivalent in her relationships as well, wanting to be her own person but frequently hooking up with those she felt were more capable than her. Then she would become too emotionally dependent upon them and struggle with the competing emotions of feeling dominated and the fear she didn't have what it would take to chart her own course. But she's no longer the same person she once was, and that's definitely for the better. She was able to learn from the empowerment she felt after asserting herself in her job search and to generalize what she learned to her relationships as well. She is living proof that making changes in behavior patterns can lead to profound changes in attitudes, thinking patterns, and even personality characteristics.

Among all the various personality types, assertiveness is arguably the healthiest type of aggression. That's because such personalities have reckoned with their anxieties, insecurities, and unhealthy dependencies and declared a sort of emotional and interpersonal independence. Assertive personalities actively take care of themselves in a way that still respects the rights and needs of others. In so doing, within their relationships they find avenues for mutual support as opposed to falling into patterns of codependence. But assertive personalities aren't born that way, nor do they become assertive overnight. They have to practice assertive behavior, and that usually involves using the tools: decide, plan, then act.

***

To be assertive: decide, plan, and then act.

***

Aggressive vs. Assertive Behavior

Assertive behavior is a type of aggressive behavior in the world of psychological terminology, but assertiveness is also key element to healthy, independent, adult functioning. But because asserting oneself is a form of "fighting" for one's legitimate needs, it's easy to get confused between the difference of what we typically understand to be "aggressive" and "assertive" in our everyday language.

There have always been so many misconceptions about the nature of aggression. First, many equate aggression with violence, when nothing could be further from the truth. The vast majority of aggressive behavior among human beings is not violent. Second, the many different forms aggression can take were poorly understood or confused, as exemplified by how often terms like passive aggression are misused—discussed in the last chapter.

Aggression in human beings is not synonymous with violence. Human aggression is the forceful energy we all expend to survive, prosper, and secure the things we want or need. We reflect a deep-seeded awareness of this fact in our language. We say things like, "If you really want something, you have to fight for it" or "If you aren't afraid of the outcome, then it's not worth fighting for." We encourage those who are sick or infirmed to do battle with their cancer, infection, or other disease. As a society, we even launched a "war on poverty."

Fighting, as discussed in the last chapter, is a huge part of life, but how and we fight is another matter entirely. And here there are big differences between aggression and assertion. Assertive behavior is fighting for a legitimate purpose. It's fair and it's principled. It's done with deliberately imposed and observed limits. The rights and boundaries of others are respected. The assertive person rejects violence and seeks a constructive goal, one that will make the situation better.

In contrast, unhealthy aggressive behavior is fighting for a purely selfish interest and to simply gain advantage over another. No care is taken to impose limits or restraints, and the rights and boundaries of others are of little concern. The goal is destructive because the goal is to weaken or incapacitate an opponent, and this can often involve violence.

It's important to understand the various ways people fight with one another and how to protect and empower yourself. Learning how to stand up for your legitimate wants and needs without trampling the rights of others and without undue apprehension about the right kind of fighting is at the heart of personal empowerment and healthy confrontation.

How to Break a Vicious Cycle: Target the Weakest Link

Once you'd had the *Aha!* and you have decided that things can be different in your relationship, you are ready to plan and then act with assertiveness. This means that you have found your best leverage point to bring about healthy change, which is vital in vicious cycles of distress, especially in your relationship with a disturbed character.

Your best course of action is to target the weakest link and stop the cycle before it escalates out of control.

***

Stop the cycle before it escalates out of control.

***

Vicious cycles of self-defeat occur in unhealthy relationships, especially relationships with disturbed characters. And although I've spent a whole career attempting to empower folks with tools they can use to chart a better course, many times it seems they're hesitant to use those tools on what they think is "just little stuff." But when you're in a seriously unhealthy or abusive relationship, little stuff typically leads to bigger stuff, and it's not uncommon for situations to escalate out of control before you know it. It's important to break those vicious cycles at the weakest point in the behavior chain. That would mean, for example, enforcing a boundary and disengaging with someone at the first offensive verbal barrage they go on, rather than waiting until things have escalated to the point of vile name-calling, shouting, and threatening.

Vicious cycles are quite simple to break. The reason this doesn't always seem easy is, not so much because they don't have a weak link (all cycles do), but because folks don't place enough importance on taking action early. In the case of anxiety disorders, this is often because the person hasn't yet adequately trained themselves in the art of spotting the subtlest, weakest anxiety signs early in the cycle. In the case of problem relationships, it's generally because the long-suffering and enduring person in an abusive situation hasn't yet come to appreciate the supreme value of immediate self-assertion as opposed to tolerating in the hopes things will get better on their own. But whether you struggle with anxiety or you're in a relationship with a difficult person, it would behoove you to take note of the vicious cycles that often fuel your difficulties and commit to breaking them at their earliest, weakest point.

Being a Non-anxious Presence

Being a cool, calm, unflappable, non-anxious presence is a mark of assertive behavior, and it is helpful in any stressful situation or conflict especially when dealing with disturbed characters. People who act assertively, with mature character are those who have learned to manage their anxiety. And we have all witnessed that a non-anxious presence is an invaluable asset during any conflict. Many therapists and those in counseling professions work toward behaving in this way, because it is helpful to clients. So it is important to look at anything that interferes and causes us to be anxious. Being anxious undercuts any assertive behavior.

You may want to be a non-anxious presence and act assertively with the disturbed people you know, but you may also be crippled by anxiety, or the disturbed person in your life might suffer from an anxiety disorder. All of us have experienced anxiety at some time or another. And in just the right doses, sometimes anxiety can actually benefit us, helping us mentally prepare for important or challenging tasks, making us take caution when it's prudent to do so, and even heightening our ability to learn. But excessive anxiety can overwhelm and debilitate anyone. And there are individuals who, for various reasons, experience anxiety on a level that painfully interferes with their ability to carry on the activities of normal daily life. For these people who suffer from the various types of anxiety disorders, fear and worry can paralyze.

Anxiety, the Enemy of Assertiveness

Long before I began specializing in the areas of personality and character disturbance, a principal focus of my therapy practice was helping people overcome anxiety and panic to become a non-anxious presence. The psychological research on anxiety disorders and their treatment is quite rich and has yielded perhaps more practical, useful, and proven methods for helping folks overcome these types of problems than any other mental health malady. Having been trained in a wide variety of methods, some of which were just proving themselves to be the treatments of choice, and having struggled with anxiety problems of my own earlier in life, I was eager to help people whose lives were negatively impacted by their various anxiety-related disorders.

One of the most important things one eventually has to learn about managing anxiety is that its symptoms and a person's typical response to them most often fuel a vicious cycle (or vicious circle) of events. If this goes unchecked it can lead to high levels of distress. Most of the time, these cycles take place under the radar of a person's conscious attention. They are just part of normal life, so they escape attention, and the person doesn't have a chance to appreciate their role in the panic that might eventually ensue. A typical scenario might go like this: A woman struggles with panic attacks and agoraphobia (i.e., literally, "fear of the marketplace" or fear of being in open spaces or among crowds); she notices she is out of milk and needs to drive to the store for more. She experiences a bit of anxiety related to what to do, and that anxiety fuels some negative self-talk about the last time she had to go out and drive somewhere alone. As she reaches the door, she experiences a few palpitations; then she begins to anticipate the other symptoms she might experience, remembering the last time she had a panic attack while going to the store. She hesitates for a moment, and when she entertains the thought of just staying home, her palpitations calm down. This reinforces her idea that going out will be a disaster (and exemplifies the fact that most agoraphobic panic suffers don't actually fear the market itself but rather, they fear the distress they expect to experience in that environment). Later, she tries again and almost makes it to the car before she is overcome by a wave of panic. She tries using the strategies her therapist taught her, but the waves of panic keep coming. She remembers she didn't feel this way when she was safe in the house, makes a bee line for the door, then the couch and remains there the rest of the day. She has no palpitations, no fears of dying or losing control, but she also has no milk.

One of the most important lessons to be learned from a story like the one above is that, even though a person's therapist might have given them tools to manage their anxiety and despite the therapist having modeled non-anxious presence for them, it's almost always too late to start using them effectively once a full-blown panic occurs. The spiraling interplay of thoughts, nervous system responses, and avoidance behaviors have already cycled to a fever pitch by the time panic sets in. So, the best time to use the tools is at the first moment one experiences any apprehension at all (e.g., when the woman in the story first notices she's out of milk and begins thinking about the reality that she might have to venture out to the store). It's much easier to break a vicious cycle when you break the chain of escalating events at its weakest (and most often, earliest) link.

According to statistics provided by the National Institute of Mental Health, researchers have found that approximately eighteen percent of adults and twenty-five percent of children and adolescents have experienced debilitating anxiety at some point during their lifetime. And a significant proportion of these individuals have been diagnosed with an anxiety disorder classified as severe enough to greatly impact their ability to function adaptively in the home and working life. The symptoms of anxiety can be quite distressing. They can include such sensations as feeling like your heart is pounding or racing, being cold yet sweating in the extremities, feeling apprehensive and jittery, having dry mouth, feeling short of breath, trembling, dizziness, and nausea. And because the symptoms themselves are so unnerving, many times anxiety over the symptoms actually increases a person's distress. It's a vicious cycle that's hard to break without professional intervention.

We All Get Anxious

We all have anxiety, but how we manage our anxiety makes all the difference. And whereas some once thought anxiety disorders were a manifestation of weakness in one's character, we have known for some time that there are many factors that contribute to the development of such conditions, including a family predisposition toward such illnesses, a person's biological makeup, certain developmental and personality factors, and abnormalities in brain functioning and neurotransmitter chemical balances. For some, the various biological factors are so influential that anxiety can occur in relatively stress-free circumstances, whereas for others, problems surface when stress levels have become high. But in any case, having an anxiety disorder is not a sign of weakness, but rather an indication of a neurobiological system out of tilt.

As distressing as the various anxiety disorders can be to experience, there is good news for sufferers, in that most can be effectively treated with proper intervention. In fact, treatment for anxiety disorders enjoys one of the highest intervention success rates of any of the various psychological maladies. Sometimes treatment involves only the use of medications. Other times, non-chemical therapies are employed. Many times, it's a combination of medication and various psychotherapies, especially cognitive-behavioral therapy (CBT) that proves the most effective course. Treatment can be relatively circumscribed and time-limited, or in some cases, more long-term. There's a variety of options, all of which have demonstrated effectiveness, and certain of which appear more appropriate for particular conditions.

I have worked with individuals suffering from anxiety disorders, especially panic disorder. And long before research had emerged that supported the notion, it became apparent to me that those caught in the trap of avoiding certain situations (e.g., going to school, driving a car, going to the supermarket, etc.) weren't so much fearful of the places *per se*, but rather fearful of experiencing the dreaded anxiety symptoms they had grown to anticipate might occur in those places. And long before CBT became popular and had research support for its effectiveness, I had the good fortune to witness many individuals use the strategies of changing their thoughts and actions to break the vicious cycle of panic escalation. The science of treatment for anxiety has improved considerably since those early days, and there is every reason for a person paralyzed by intense or irrational fears to have hope that proper intervention will help free them to enjoy life once again.

Take Away

Before people can behave differently and act assertively, they must experience the consequences, then "see" the errors of their former ways. Not only do people have to practice different behavior, they also need a lot of reinforcement for doing things differently. *Aha!* moments come along with doing the new behavior repeatedly, and to learn to be assertive means that one practices following these steps:

1. Decide

2. Plan

3. Act

Assertive behavior means that we remain a non-anxious presence, because unmanaged anxiety undercuts our assertiveness and our ability to deal effectively with the disturbed people in our lives.

Empowerment Tools

1. It's not so much seeing as doing that usually creates the most powerful *Aha!* moments in our lives.

2. When learning the art of healthy confrontation, it is important to remember that the ability to act non-defensively and with objectivity calls for assertive behavior.

3. To foster an assertive personality, actively taking care of yourself in a way that still respects the rights and needs of others, means applying these simple steps: decide, plan, then act.

4. Sometimes before you can confront someone, you have to overcome your own obstacles, so that you can be appropriately assertive.

Chapter Four
The Art of Healthy Confrontation

The Power of Confrontation

Confrontation is difficult for many people, and because of this we hesitate, even though the results can be powerful. Those of us in the helping professions have also been reluctant to engage in any kind of confrontation with clients. The main reason for this stems largely from assumptions flowing from the more traditional psychology paradigms—paradigms that are neither as appropriate nor as useful in our present age of more pervasive character disturbance.

But confrontation is often necessary especially with disturbed characters. As I assert in *Character Disturbance*, no problem has ever been successfully ameliorated in therapy until it's been correctly identified (and also correctly labeled) and appropriately confronted. But it's in the **artful** manner that we confront the various problems needing attention that has the power to make genuine change possible. The problem is that once you confront someone, the person has to acknowledge you and accept what you have to say. In some way they have to admit that they are powerless and thus willing to change. This is always the first step in any Twelve-Step program, but you can't even get there until you call out the problem, the proverbial elephant in the room.

Correctly identifying the problem—not merely the surface-level manifestations of the problem but also its root cause—is what diagnosis is all about. In my books and workshops, I continually say that intervention in the absence of sound diagnosis is the very definition of malpractice. You have to know what's really going on with someone, why it's going on, and what the best means of addressing it is, if you're going to be of genuine help. Defining the problem, its cause, and what needs to be done to correct it is what therapeutic confrontation is all about.

***

**Artful confrontation is powerful and
can make genuine change possible.**

***

But knowing what the problem is and then confronting someone about it doesn't have to be reserved for professionals. There are times in any relationship when confrontation is helpful and necessary. But the principle remains. To reap the reward and the power that confrontation can bring, the problem has to be correctly identified. But just because you've correctly identified a problem and know what needs to be done about it, doesn't mean things will necessarily get better. There are a lot of other variables that enter into that equation, not the least of which is a person's willingness to accept the diagnosis and comply with the recommended intervention. But a person's reluctance to own their pathology and commit themselves to the recommended treatment strategy should never be a reason not call out a problem for exactly what it is. This is the mistake so often made by clinicians overly aligned with traditional perspectives. When it comes to someone's pathology, helping professionals are obliged to call it right and address it properly, even in the face of possible resistance. Certainly resistance can and should be dealt with. And sometimes, a person's resistance can be really difficult if not impossible to overcome. But that shouldn't be a license for a therapist to either "candy-coat" or otherwise misrepresent a problem and what really needs to be done about it.

Without Confrontation Problems Remain

For far too long, the notion of confronting someone, especially within the context of a therapy session, carried negative connotations. But to reiterate: the reality is that no problem has ever been solved, until it has been directly confronted, including problems involving a person's behavior. So the secret to helping people change is not to avoid confrontation altogether, but to ensure that when you confront, you do so in a manner that gets to the heart of issues without unduly disparaging or alienating the person with the behavioral problems; and therein lies the art of healthy confrontation.

***

Healthy confrontation gets to the heart of issues without unduly disparaging or alienating the person with the behavioral problems.

***

Like many therapists, I was initially trained to avoid creating a climate that might invite a client to unconsciously raise their defenses and therefore shy away from developing that all-important therapeutic relationship. In that regard, there were some things a therapist just wasn't supposed to do: ask direct, probing "why" questions; make interpretations about a person's behavior that reflected a judgment about the moral character of those behaviors; or put someone on the "defensive" by calling direct attention to (and therefore exposing) their less functional way of coping. Instead, therapists were supposed to primarily display compassion for the hurt, which must surely and necessarily underlie their maladaptive behavior; build a trusting, empathic bond; and then slowly and systematically help the person "work through" both their feelings and their issues. And of course, you would never say something as direct and potentially provocative as: "It appears you think of yourself as entirely too special, and this causes problems in your relationships." Not only because that is an inherently negative, hurtful thing to say; but also because, while it may be true that the person acts in a haughty way, they're presumed to be unaware of what they're doing. The assumption is that the person feels insecure and inferior underneath it all, and confrontation would only lead to unhelpful shame and guilt; therefore inhibiting the healing process. By saying such a thing, you were only pouring salt on an already substantial wound and damaging any chance you had to form a therapeutic (healing) bond.

But after years of experience working with disturbed characters, I came to recognize two very important realities.

1. To assume that everyone's actions are driven primarily by unconscious motives and that those motives are always rooted in fears and insecurities is folly.

2. When you don't confront a character-impaired person on what they already know they're doing, they not only hold you in low regard (sometimes even in disdain or contempt), but they deem you both untrustworthy and easily manipulated.

As a result, I began to craft a manner of confronting that was direct yet clearly devoid of hostility—a matter-of-fact, dispassionate way of calling of attention to behaviors of concern, coupled with both encouragement and reinforcement for a person's willingness to take a different course.

People often say that they were once afraid to confront their emotionally abusive relationship partners for the same reasons therapists have avoided confrontation. "I was afraid he'd feel attacked. And on past occasions when I did say something, he'd act offended and get all defensive, making me feel really bad about having said anything at all," one woman reported. The problem is that in backing down from confrontation, and especially in buying into the notion that the abusive party is both unaware of what they're doing and primarily struggling with fears and insecurities, the aggrieved party inevitably ends up tolerating, and thus "enabling" problem behaviors to continue. Moreover, if the parties just happened to seek counseling from a therapist firmly aligned with traditional perspectives, such a pattern is likely to get heavily reinforced, and neither person will get the help they really need. I've witnessed this kind of thing happening time and time again.

***

Backing down from confrontation enables problem behaviors to continue.

***

Recently, a gentleman contacted me who had been involved in couples counseling with a therapist familiar with the newer perspectives and well versed in the art of healthy confrontation.

> At first, I was stunned when she (the therapist) confronted my now ex on her behavior. My ex acted so outraged when confronted that I immediately thought to myself: "The therapist has gone too far, and now I'm actually feeling sorry for her, because she's wounded and feels like I've been a party to an attack on her." But to my surprise, the therapist got her to admit not only what she was doing, but also that the outrage she displayed was just a tactic to make us question ourselves and back off. In that moment, I came to see her and our whole relationship in an entirely different light.

I've gotten reports similar to this from hundreds of individuals over the years, and it's always edifying to learn of someone's positive experience with the process of healthy confrontation.

We all know that life is complicated and relationships are messy and need careful attention. But some issues are harder to deal with than others, especially when it comes to human behavior. Sometimes we have good intentions and sometimes we're lazy. No two people are alike, and no one can always predict how someone will respond. But no problem has ever been solved without first being identified and then confronted head-on. That's why, in the age of character disturbance, perhaps there's no more necessary or valuable practice.

But sometimes a person just has to learn the hard way. When Juan's (name and significant details altered) relationship partner took a serious look at him, she didn't at all like what she saw. On the other hand, when Juan looked in the mirror, he was more than pleased with himself. When it comes to personality and character patterns, many times the very aspects of a person's makeup that trouble others are not only acceptable to but also fondly embraced by the person possessing them.

Professionals call this *egosyntonia*. There are certainly occasions when a person is actually troubled by certain aspects of their own personality. They might actually even hate the way they react in various situations, but because they don't seem to be able to help themselves, they're miserable about it. In short, they're not really comfortable with the person they are. We call this *egodystonia*. But most of the time, where significant character disturbance is present, the person with the disturbance likes who they are, prefers the way they feel and think about things, is quite comfortable with the way they do things, and believes, not only that everyone else has a problem but also, that the world would be a better place if everyone else thought, felt, and acted just as they do. Juan was one of this type of person.

Juan didn't like what I, his therapist, had to say about him and the nature of his problems. And more than being non-receptive, he sought to challenge me on my diagnosis at every turn. He relentlessly fought to get me to back down or change my mind. But while I was sure of the diagnosis and the intervention that would be necessary, I couldn't make Juan embrace either, so I was prepared to let him go and discontinue his treatment. However, Juan was an interesting case, because he actually wanted to stay and fight (to get me to change my mind) and in response, I had to firmly deny him access. I remain certain that sending Juan away and refusing to see him was the most potentially therapeutic thing I could have done at the time. And just because I sent him packing didn't mean my door would remain closed to a Juan more willing to accept reality.

That day did come, because as fate would have it, life ended up teaching Juan some hard lessons. And when he was in a better place—a more humble (i.e., "defeated"), open, and amenable place—and really wanted help. I'm clear that he came back to see me, because unlike the several other therapists he'd been dragged to see in the past, I "dared" (his words) to name his problem for what it really was (i.e., pathological ego-inflation). It wasn't that he had "problems with communication," or "commitment fears," or "deep-seated insecurities," or any of the many other fancy-sounding but mark-missing conditions suggested to him in the past. He was simply a man who thought far too much of himself and carried such a huge sense of entitlement into every relationship that he was always causing shipwrecks. And when he finally stopped kidding himself, because he never forgot what I told him the problem was, he became hungry enough for something more out of life. He knew that he needed guidance to suitably reshape himself, and so he sought out someone he thought he could trust. Juan also came with the positive expectation (shown by mounds of research to be the single most important factor for successful therapy outcome) that I would help him. And I firmly believe that's because even though I "dared" confront him (and pretty strongly as I remember) he still did not sense in me any malicious intent to wound, demean, or condemn him, but rather a sincere desire to support his growth.

I've experienced scenarios like the kind I've described with Juan time and time again. But I've also encountered plenty of folks who, unlike Juan, remained so prideful, stubborn, and self-satisfied that they possibly went to their graves the same disturbed character they'd always been. But I've met a lot more folks like Juan—people who appeared almost impossible to deal with at the time and who I simply had to let go—and I'm grateful I learned relatively early on how to be at peace with wherever a person is at the moment with respect to their personal growth.

Even when we say, "You're just like your mother" or "You tell that story just like Uncle Jack," we really don't mean it. We all know that no two people are exactly alike, and that same principle applies to disturbed characters as well. No two are alike and, to complicate matters further, disturbances exist along a continuum, a spectrum. Just as there are light and severe cases of strep throat, there are less severe and more severe cases of psychological disturbance. This fact is important, because there is virtually no hope for those characters that are extremely disturbed, at least with currently available methods of treatment.

Earlier I mentioned the old joke about two female social workers on the streets of Manhattan who got their purses snatched by a mugger on a bicycle and then give chase shouting: "Stop that man! Stop him! He clearly needs our help!" And I had to learn the hard way how, not only disrespectful but also counter-therapeutic, it is to try and help someone who's neither asking for help nor is particularly open to it. As disrespectful, "enabling," and counterproductive bad behavior can be, I doubt there's anything more damaging as refusing to call out a problem for what it really is. But while it was difficult to learn, I did learn how to confront in a healthy, therapeutic, healthy way. And you can too.

The Structure of Healthy Confrontation

Diagnosis helps define the problem and, consequently, it also determines the type of therapeutic intervention. Diagnosis gives the therapist the prescribed path toward greater health for the client. This means that one only undertakes a course of action that necessarily impacts someone's life in a significant way with a scientifically well-founded rational. Think about it for a minute. Would you seriously consider going back to a dentist who, upon your first visit, suggested that you allow him or her to simply start drilling your teeth, just to see what they find and then confer an opinion later? I think not. You'd probably prefer that some examination was done to determine exactly what the nature of your problem was and then be apprised of the generally accepted remedy for dealing with that problem before you give consent. The same is true for psychological and behavioral problems. Before intervening, you have to know with some reasonable level of certainty exactly what the problem is and what's causing it, because that in large measure points dictates the course of action you most likely need to take to resolve the problem.

***

Diagnosis gives the prescribed path toward greater health for the client.

***

I'm not exactly sure how the term "confrontation" garnered such negative connotations or how the act of confronting—even confronting benignly and therapeutically—got such a bad rap. But I know that traditional psychological paradigms had us all believing that most of the time, people do things with little conscious awareness about their underlying motivations. And these same paradigms also taught us that underneath it all, we all want the same things, have the same wants, needs, desires, etc. We thought that while we might be misguided about how to secure these things, our basic desires are good and pure, and to call attention in a way that seems judgmental to the unhealthy ways we might tend to seek these things, would inevitably only prompt a person to become both defensive, uncooperative, and possibly damage their self-esteem.

In my early professional training, I observed a therapy session with a married couple whose relationship was on the brink. And each time one partner complained about the verbally abusive, denigrating language the other partner frequently used, that partner would justify the behavior by asserting such language wouldn't be necessary if the other partner would simply see things correctly (i.e., their way) and not provoke their ire. The therapist, in turn, would ask the partner making the justifications to search their feelings for the underlying fears or concerns giving rise to their anger and venting of hostility. Meanwhile, the abuse continued, often and unabated. Later, during a debriefing session, I was shocked when the therapist rightfully made the observation that the one partner showed both a degree of haughtiness and entitlement that was truly troubling, and I had the naiveté to ask why that wasn't confronted directly. Of course, the answer was: "Oh, you can't do that! Your client will get so defensive they'll just shut down, or perhaps they'll even stop coming. That won't get you anywhere."

The therapist and I also discussed how he viewed the problem. "Communication issues," and more specifically, "communication issues stemming from unresolved fears and wounds in childhood" was the response. After all, would a person behave so callously to the person they purported to love and without much apparent empathy or remorse? So week after week, the couple would come in and work on communicating better and processing the feelings they were having that gave rise to their frustrations. This continued for many months with even worse verbal berating when the couple was at home, but what really made a dent in the cycle of relational abuse was one party finally having enough, deciding to get out and file for divorce.

I reflected on this case long and hard before coming to some conclusions that, at the time, were considered more than a bit radical but are generally better accepted today. And one of the more important things I decided had to do with what was and was not properly confronted during the sessions I observed. A clinician has to determine exactly what the main problem is, the root of it, and what would have to be done to ameliorate it, if that's even possible. And in this case, I determined that "communication" was not in itself the problem or the root any of the couple's problems. Rather, I saw the kind of communication one partner was repeatedly willing to engage in as a cardinal sign (cardinal signs are objectively observable manifestations of a condition or disorder that are so indicative of one condition as opposed to another that their mere presence is both a strong and reliable predictor that someone has a particular disorder). I added up all the signs and symptoms: grandiosity, feelings of entitlement, repeated violations of boundaries without sufficient compunction or apparent remorse, and decided that the more fundamental and primary diagnosis was one of Narcissistic Personality Disorder (NPD).

At the time, the field of psychology was truly in a quandary about how to best intervene with character disturbances, especially NPD, with many insisting, as some still do today, that when it comes to personality or character disorders, there is no effective treatment. For me, this was the beginning of a period of investigation and theoretical reorientation that would eventually define my career.

My experience has only solidified a perspective I came to quite some time ago. No problem has a chance of being successfully treated or ameliorated until and unless it's

1. correctly identified and accurately labeled, and

2. confronted in the manner most likely to promote constructive resolution.

And within this structure, over the years, I sought to refine my own method of healthy confrontation.

Getting to the Heart of the Problem

To really help someone, you have to strip away all the superficial manifestations of the problem and get to the heart of the matter; and much of the time that points to one's character (whether a person is of a mind to admit it or not). And upon realizing how many people's problems were in some way related to a person's character disturbance (i.e., problems of their own making, arising out of their own deficiencies of character or problems caused by being in a relationship with a person of significantly disturbed character), I began to find ways to give the average person a framework for understanding the true nature of the problems we so frequently encounter, and how such problems really need to be addressed both at the interpersonal and professional level if they're ever to have a chance at resolve.

***

Many problems are related to a person's character disturbance.

***

The Art of Loving and Healthy Confrontation

I first read Erich Fromm's landmark work, *The Art of Loving*, when I was studying philosophy and psychology in college. I must confess that at the time, being both a naïve and yet somewhat presumptuous young man, I didn't fully appreciate its content or message. In fact, at the time, I found parts of it trite and misguidedly idealistic. I read it again in graduate school not once, but twice, to satisfy the demands of two different professors. Each professor promoted a slightly different perspective on helping people change, but both still attested to the important role a wholesome relationship can play in guiding someone toward greater emotional, psychological, and spiritual health. But only after years of work with difficult and problematic characters did I fully get it with respect to the power of skilled, artful loving, and the vital role it can play in the amelioration of human suffering.

Genuine regard for a person's well-being can't be just a matter of sentiment. Fromm emphasizes this same point. And although it's certainly important for therapists to have a deep sense of empathy and to care about those with whom they work, when intervening with those of significantly impaired character, both positive and negative sentiments can at times be serious impediments to fostering therapeutic change and personal growth. As Fromm so eloquently makes the case, really loving—especially loving the disturbed character—requires these actions: incredible discipline, patience, interaction skill, artful technique, and most important, courage to confront. And as I have learned after many years of doing some of the most difficult work, confronting an individual on their distorted thinking and problematic behavior patterns in a fully honest, forthright—yet non-hostile, non-resentful, and truly healthy—way requires a most demanding skill set, and when done tactfully, arguably rises to the level of a genuine art.

There are many practical benefits to honest and healthy confrontation. For one, confrontation based upon principles of pro-social conduct bespeak, at least to some degree, one's own character and level of integrity. For another, displaying an unwavering commitment to one's principles and displaying the courage of one's convictions during healthy confrontations lay the foundation for the most essential element of any potentially therapeutic relationship: trust. And focusing like a laser beam on the destructive aspects of someone's modes of thinking and behavior, while demonstrating an unwavering commitment to respecting their worth as a person, provides an extremely attractive avenue to greater interpersonal communion.

Perhaps the most important lesson I learned from Fromm that carried into my work is the importance behaving with proper self-love. And keeping a commitment to myself not to engage with people in any manner that ultimately abuses, denigrates, or exploits them, empowered me to establish the boundaries and enforce the limits necessary to foster here-and-now change within the therapeutic relationship.

Character Disturbance and the Art of Confrontation

I get dozens of emails every year from folks asking how to effectively confront disturbed characters about their behavior. Sometimes they fear an unhealthy defensive or coping response on the part of the person confronted or possibly even a vindictive or destructive retaliatory response. But confrontation can be the most loving thing a person can do for a relationship. Below are some general, helpful rules that can really assist a person in the art of healthy, powerful confrontation.

***

Confrontation can be the most loving thing a person can do for a relationship.

***

But something else needs to be made clear from the outset. There is nothing inherently provocative or detrimental about confrontation. True, one can spark conflict by engaging in aggressive, hostile, confrontation. But the essence of confrontation lies in meeting or addressing an issue or problem head-on as opposed to dancing all around it. And we expect nothing less than this kind of laser-beam type focus when we're confronting social problems like poverty and injustice. Confrontation, done well, ensures that the spotlight falls where its light needs to shine the most: directly on a behavior of concern.

How one goes about confronting the issues in a dysfunctional relationship is another matter entirely. When it comes to dealing with disturbed characters, truly **artful confrontation is a must**. For the sake of clarity and simplicity, here are the four most important rules:

First, be sure of the need. Many times, people have it in their heads that it's their responsibility to point out to the disturbed character in their life what that person is doing wrong, so they will see the light and then modify their behavior. This, of course, assumes that the person doesn't already know what they're doing or why they're doing it, and will somehow be motivated to take a different course if someone just points things out to them. But disturbed characters are usually well-aware. What they need—and more important, what you need to empower yourself—are firmly established limits on behavior. And it's simply not necessary to "red flag" the behavior you want to target, limit, and change.

To illustrate this point, here is an example with which many introductory psychology students exploring the realms of behavior theory are familiar. A class of students asks one student to leave the classroom and remain in the hallway while the others decide upon a special task. The class decides that the secret target task will be to have the student, upon re-entering the classroom, place their foot in a trash can at the front of the room. The only clues they will offer the "guinea pig" in this experiment about what is expected will be to clap (more loudly or softly) as the person tries out various behaviors in an attempt to figure out what the class wants him or her to do. Then the person enters the classroom. As the guinea pig moves around from location to location, clapping ensues in various degrees of intensity and frequency, getting louder and/or more frequent as the person moves nearer the trash can. It becomes even more pronounced as the person experiments with various types of activities near and about the trash can, eventually erupting into a roar of approval when the person tests out placing a leg in the can. No one had to tell this person what to do or to spell out the behavior that was expected. As those versed in behavior theory know, behavior is influenced by its consequences.

Anyone can figure out what is expected, when the expectations are made clear and consequences (in the form of recognition or reward or withdrawal of recognition or reward) are put into place. This is called shaping behavior. The important thing to remember is that the most effective way to target a behavior is to make sure that the expectations, limits, and consequences are clear. If you are dealing with someone who simply refuses to modify their behavior despite clear limits, expectations, and consequences, you're probably in a situation you're best getting miles away from as opposed to wasting time and energy confronting the person, because you will be confronting that person all the time.

Second, when you do confront, take all the emotion out of it. Strive to be a non-anxious presence. It's easy for focus to get lost when attention is diverted to one's own emotional responses—or anything else for that matter. So you have to do your best to remain calm, cool, and collected. Besides, it's easier to think clearly when you're not worked up. The ideal time to confront is when there is absolutely nothing except the behavior in question that anyone can point to as the issue that needs attention. This needs to be clear. It's not about me as a person, and it's not about you as a person; it's not about my feelings or your feelings; it's about a particular behavior, pure and simple.

Disturbed personalities are always looking for an excuse to go to war. So they will see any hostility, sarcasm, or put-down as an attack, thus making them feel justified in launching an offensive. Do not attack their character, but also don't back away from confrontation, just be sure to confront in a way that is up-front yet non-aggressive. Confronting without maligning or denigrating is not only an art but a necessary skill in dealing with disturbed characters.

Third, don't wait. When a problem behavior occurs, address it quickly. Behavior often occurs in patterns or "chains," and disturbed characters frequently exhibit destructive escalations of their behavior when those chains progress in an uninterrupted fashion. The time to walk out of the room is when the first verbal character assault is hurled in response to your addressing the problem. Things can get ever so much more risky if you allow yourself to think that you can simply wait until the insults get "bad enough" that you simply have to do something in response. If you really want the spotlight to shine on a behavior, respond to it the very moment it first occurs. And if you don't want things to escalate, you'll establish a track record of responding reliably and quickly to a problem behavior.

Four, confrontation can bring risks, but it can also be your most powerful tool for change. Disturbed characters do not take the answer "no" easily, and there is almost always a price to pay for enforcing a limit. Be aware that in the more problematic situations, the most dangerous time is when the limits are most clearly defined and enforced. That's another reason why it's so important to address behavior issues early on and to enter relationships with a focus *from* *the beginning* on empowering oneself as educating and improving the behavior of the other person.

An Eye for an Eye: Reciprocal Justice or Perpetual Injustice?

Confrontation is one answer to the question about how best to secure justice and respond to injury. This issue is as old as time. And despite the more esoteric, intellectual thinking to the contrary that might occur in college classrooms or in dinner table discussions, the stark reality is that the adage "eye-for-an-eye, tooth-for-a-tooth" still dominates the mentality of most aggrieved individuals and even countries. This prescription for addressing injustice has been with us even since the days of Hammurabi's Code and the Torah. But the primary intention of these ancient writings was to prevent an injured party from exacting outrageous, excessive retribution from the alleged perpetrator (as well as the offender's family) of an offense, while also attempting to ensure that victims were not deprived of fair and adequate compensation for losses they might have suffered. So the principle is really about a measured approach to seeking and meting out justice. But the more common mentality arising from this perspective has too often been a "you have smitten me so now I shall smite you" approach to settling scores. And history tells us that this approach does little to balance competing interests while doing a lot to perpetuate or even escalate conflict.

Gandhi is reported to have said that "an eye for an eye makes the whole world blind." There is wisdom on multiple levels to this statement. After lengthy stints of mutual retaliation, people tend, to not only lose sight of what they've really been fighting for, but they also lose their ability to find more constructive alternatives. It's sad, unfortunate, inordinately self-defeating, but nonetheless all too common. Conflict can breed retaliation, thus perpetuating cycles of violence. And so it goes, on and on—the very definition of insanity is doing the same thing over and over again, yet expecting different results.

As is the case in most conflicts, each side has legitimate needs and aspirations. However if the participants can avoid severely thwarting or ignoring each other's needs and aspirations, the fuel necessary to exacerbate a conflict is greatly diminished. That's why true practitioners of healthy confrontation strive to discover, respect, and attend to the legitimate concerns of all parties. This is as true for international diplomacy these days, as it is for personal relationships. Confrontation is not retaliation, a way to seek revenge, or giving a person what they deserve. Rather it is a responsible means to break the cycle of bad behavior and draw appropriate and just boundaries.

Fear Can Be a Real Concern

One major obstacle to confrontation is just plain fear and sometimes rightly so. Manipulators and other disturbed characters sometimes like to openly threaten or brow-beat someone else into giving-up or giving-in to their demands. This can make confrontation difficult and sometimes impossible. These disturbed persons like to terrorize others into submission. They use your fear as a weapon against you, whether it's fear of the known or unknown. People in relationships with disturbed characters are generally familiar with their track record of behavior, thus they know what the disturbed character is not only capable of, but also what they have been willing to do to get their way in the past.

Disturbed characters can bully and manipulate others by keeping them on the defensive, making them so afraid of possible negative repercussions that they don't dare go against the bully's wishes. Sometimes, they will brandish intense anger and rage, not so much because they're really that angry, but because they want their victims to be so terrorized that they dare not do anything but cave in to their demands. That doesn't mean that victims should take the behavior of their tormentors lightly, it simply means that they have to recognize that they are in an unhealthy relationship with a person who will stop at nothing to get his or her way.

Individuals who frequently use bullying as a manipulation tactic are among the least likely to change their *modus operandi*. That's because in addition to being an effective tactic of manipulation, such hard-headed combativeness is also a primary way the disturbed character avoids any kind of submission to a higher authority or standard of conduct. Those who refuse to subjugate themselves to anything wage a constant war against the internalization of standards and controls that make most of us civilized. Suffice it to say that the best idea is to not remain in any kind of relationship with a person willing to engage in such behavior.

I once consulted with an organization in which there was a mid-level manager who quickly took charge of any situation she was faced with and generally did well for her company. But she also struck fear into the hearts of those who dared question or oppose her. Many a co-worker experienced premature burnout working with or for her. One of her supervisors remarked to me that he knew she must be "a frightened, insecure child underneath," and he therefore coached others that the "psychological secret" to getting along with her was to be both non-threatening and reassuring. But this woman was a ruthless albeit covert power seeker. She was driven neither by fear nor insecurity but rather an insatiable appetite (more accurately, lust) for power and control.

There are those among us who are by nature dominance-seeking to an unhealthy extreme. Such folks crave the power position, and not because they fear being victimized if they allow themselves to be vulnerable, but because they innately abhor taking on a subordinate or submissive role. They create problems in relationships (at work and within marriages) because they simply won't allow themselves to back down, back off, or concede, even if doing so in the short run would help them emerge victorious in the long run. They're often prematurely and unnecessarily combative as opposed to defensive in their interpersonal relations. And not only do they not aggress primarily out of fear, but they are aggressive even when they're not even angry. This is the phenomenon known as instrumental (alternately: predatory) aggression, which I will describe later in some detail. Some aggressors wage war purely for the purpose of securing something, and often conduct the fight in such a stealthy manner that the victim doesn't even know they've been in a battle until they're already defeated.

When Anger Destroys:
Anger Management vs. Character Development

While fear might be a legitimate concern, what do you do with the anger you may feel or that you might ignite as you confront someone? People with aggressive personality styles are frequently already operating in an aggressive mode long before they ever become angry. For them, brandishing anger is more of an intimidation tactic than a genuine expression of emotion—and that's why many don't respond particularly well to traditional anger management interventions. Because anger is a "natural" response, it's important to discuss it in more detail.

Anger is a most misunderstood emotion. Often maligned as an evil in itself, it's one of our most basic emotions. The limbic system in our brain is designed in such a way that we can experience both fear and anger in response to an external event. Our innate survival mechanisms predispose us to "fight" or "flee" from a perceived threat, and there are some specific physiological processes that both precede and accompany these primal responses. Anger is nature's way of mobilizing us into action to remove a genuine threat to our welfare. But just as it can be problematic when our lives are characterized by too frequent or intense bouts of fear or anxiety, chronic, excessive, or mishandled, anger can also be quite destructive.

Many are familiar with the Adam Sandler's movie *Anger Management*. The lead character in the movie, Dave, has a problem. He represses his emotions, especially his anger, which causes him a great deal of difficulty in his interpersonal relationships. He is inordinately deferential to his abusive boss and overly inhibited with his girlfriend. Unbeknownst to him, his girlfriend secretly arranges for an avant-garde therapist to bring him into an unconventional "anger management" program. The therapist, Buddy (played by Jack Nicholson), makes Dave face increasingly provocative and outrageous situations, to the point that Dave finally releases his pent-up anger, though explosively; and then begins the long, arduous task of learning to better "own" and then gain control over it. And while the movie is a slapstick comedy, it contains some elements of truth about how destructive to relationships inappropriately managed anger can be.

Most genuine anger management programs operate on some well-established principles of cognitive-behavioral psychology. The leading perspective is that anger is most often the precipitant of aggressive behavior. Further, how we perceive events and think about things heavily influences not only how we feel but also how we respond; therefore most anger management therapies encourage folks who have problems with anger to challenge and change the ways they typically interpret various events in their lives. For example, if I hold the perspective that someone did something to insult me, I'm likely to respond in a much different manner than I would if I believed the person did something without malice but to which, for some reason, I took offense. How we think about and interpret events makes a big difference in how we handle our conflicts.

Having worked for years with many individuals for whom uncontrolled anger and maladaptive aggression presented problems in their interpersonal relationships, I came to realize that there is another side to the well-established notion that anger precipitates aggression. This other side must also be managed effectively if destructive interpersonal behavior is to be avoided. Individuals with aggressive personality styles (i.e., folks who fight tenaciously and unscrupulously for the things they want, as opposed to assertive individuals), are frequently already in the aggressive mode long before they ever become angry. Generally speaking, when such folks become angry, it's because they've encountered some resistance to or have been denied something they've been fighting for. And sometimes, when these personalities brandish anger, they're doing so as more of a tactic to intimidate others into giving them what they want than genuinely expressing an emotion. That's why many of these individuals don't respond all that well to typical anger management interventions. It's not their anger they really need to learn to manage most. Rather, it's their overly aggressive interpersonal style that needs attention and modification. And although programs generally referred to as "aggression replacement training" were initially tailored to the adolescent population, the basic principles of such programs are more suited to dealing with the dysfunctional style of aggressive personalities.

Chronic and poorly managed anger not only leads to destructive behavior patterns but also can significantly and negatively impact a person's health (e.g., exacerbate hypertension, coronary disease, ulcers, etc.). But it's important to first determine if someone is having more of a problem with anger management *per se* or if he has a basic personality disturbance that engenders frequent problems with anger expression. Only then can it become evident whether they need more specialized character development interventions as opposed to more traditional anger management.

Timing: An Essential Consideration

When you have decided, planned, and are ready to act, there is something else to consider: when? Whatever the state of our relationships, we still strive to keep the peace and avoid confrontation especially at holiday time. But sadly, holidays or other special family times can bring out the worst behavior. Confrontation may become necessary, but holiday time is especially stressful, so you need to ask yourself if confronting someone during, for example, the big holiday meal is what you really want to do. And it may be. Just know, however, that if you call out an elephant during this time, you are "upping the ante" and might inflict a lot of collateral damage. Or you might have the best chance of support and subsequent change if you chose a time when "everyone" is there.

Perhaps you heard the story about the legendary actress Joan Fontaine, who passed away at age ninety-six. Upon reading several articles about her life and career, I was disheartened to learn about her acrimonious relationship with her equally legendary older (by little more than a year) sister, Olivia de Havilland. The two had been at odds with each other since their early childhood, competing intensely with one another and picking fights with each other about almost everything under the sun. Over the years, they only grew further apart, failing miserably at the few feeble attempts each made at reconciling. It seemed to me such a pity that two remarkable talents, who managed to garner the love and respect of total strangers, could have so much trouble finding space in their hearts for a blood sister.

In my years of professional practice, I've unfortunately encountered many cases of estrangement among family members. None of these situations were pretty. In fact, they were downright ugly. The situations ranged from unresolved sibling rivalry to completely ostracizing a particular member, simply because that member didn't fit within the family's mold or ideal. Sometimes, the estrangement was somewhat understandable, possibly even necessary, like in cases where severe abuse and/or neglect by a parent or sibling had occurred. But other times, the distance seemed to have occurred as a result of the most trivial circumstances. Almost without exception, the estrangements were a source of great pain for the individuals affected. While that pain was with the affected parties almost all the time, it always seemed to intensify at holiday time.

Generally speaking, holidays are an occasion not only to reflect upon and celebrate one's blessings but also to enjoy the company of family and friends. They're a time, as the famous lines in the popular song *Have Yourself a Merry Little Christmas* suggest, for "faithful friends who are dear to us" to "gather near to us once more." That's what we want the holidays to be about. For example, Christmas is not just a time for exchanging gifts but a time to relish in the joy on the faces of friends and family. It's a time for catching up and sharing stories. As we share the love we have, we also pray that "through the years we all will be together." When healthy bonds are present, we naturally want to keep them strong. That's why when someone is experiencing strained relations with another family member or a once close friend during the holidays, it can be very painful indeed. Sadly, it's often pride that keeps one or both of the parties from taking that all important first step toward reconciliation, even though each might secretly desire it quite earnestly.

Holidays naturally bring with them their own special set of stresses and anxieties, and some people react to these with bad behavior. Getting all the cleaning, cooking, shopping, and decorating done is inherently stressful, as is all the traveling, planning, and arranging. But just being with the larger group of family members for extended periods of time can bring on additional stress, even when folks are on relatively good terms with one another. Sometimes, even healthy family members can fall into the trap of re-enacting old family dynamics and interaction patterns, giving rise to old anxieties and re-igniting old conflicts. Parents might even succumb to showing old patterns of favoritism, re-kindling sibling rivalries and jealousies. With families, it's easy to fall into old patterns of behavior. There is always somebody who is unhappy, even if it stems from an incident years ago. Your mother, for example, might start acting like the mean older sister, when interacting with her own siblings. Or dad might feel embarrassed to show much emotion around his father. In the end, the stress level can get pretty high during holiday get-togethers, even in the healthiest of families. Stress can easily reach toxic levels when there is severe estrangement or discord between some of the family's members. That's why it's so important to keep the spirit of the season so carefully in mind.

Fontaine and de Havilland weren't even speaking to one another in the years immediately preceding Joan's passing. As tragic as the whole circumstance is, it seems particularly sad given the time of year at which it came and the sentiments most us try to embrace as the year comes to a close. Ill feelings between family members are the surest way to put a damper on holiday cheer. If you need to confront someone, but cognizant of the fact that some times are better than others.

Take Away

Confrontation is difficult under the best of circumstances, but especially when the person being confronted has an undeveloped or disturbed character. However reluctant we might be to confront someone, it might be the most loving thing we can do for that person. And despite wishful thinking, these kinds of problems won't go away by themselves, at least for long. But there are better and worse ways to confront. Healthy confrontation focuses on the behavior, not on personal feelings—yours or the other person's. And for best results focus only on the behavior at a time when you are cool, calm, and collected—a non-anxious presence—if possible. However if you find your own fear, anxiety, and/or anger getting in the way, seek professional help. Work with someone you can trust.

Empowerment Tools

Here are the four principles of healthy confrontation:

1. Be sure of the need and your motivation to confront.

2. When you do confront, take all the emotion out of it.

3. Don't wait.

4. Confrontation can bring risks, but it can also be your most powerful tool for change.

Chapter Five
"But I'm Really Sorry": Remorse, Regret, and Contrition

We all know how the story goes. Sam and Audrey are fighting because Audrey overdrew the checking account again. No matter what Sam does or says, Audrey believes that as long as she has her debit card, she has money to spend. Their four-year marriage has been constantly rife with conflict, and each time they fight, they get louder and more violent. Sam is so frustrated that he just wants to shake some sense into Audrey. Then one time as the intensity of the fight builds, he grabs her; and she, in reaction, grabs their son's bat and hits him. Sam is so sorry. Audrey is so sorry. But nothing has really changed. They may be sorry, but neither is contrite. There'll be another fight soon.

Being Sorry Isn't Contrition

I've counseled many individuals whose problems were a direct result of deficiencies in their character and the irresponsible behavior patterns those deficiencies engendered. And while many of these individuals experienced profound periods of unhappiness and regret over their actions, only a handful ever made any significant changes in their once destructive behavior patterns. But those who did change their lives for the better displayed a rare quality that seemed to make all the difference: true contrition.

From the Latin *contritus* (the same root for the word "contrite") and literally meaning "crushed to pieces," contrition is a crushing of a person's once prideful ego under the tremendous weight of guilt and shame over the injury caused to others as a result of one's actions. It is analogous to the "hitting bottom" phenomenon that people in Twelve-Step programs experience. The contrite person is first and foremost a broken person.

Regret, or being sorry, is not the same as contrition. And when it comes to making meaningful changes in one's character and turning around an irresponsible life, regret is simply not enough. The word "regret" comes from the Old French, meaning "to bewail." It's a person's intellectual and emotional response to an unpleasant or unfortunate circumstance (originally used to characterize a person's loss of a loved one through death). Even the seasoned criminals I've counseled had regrets. They regretted the loss of their freedom. They lamented the fact that a judge was able to exercise power over them and subject them to unpleasant ordeals as a result of their actions. And while some even regretted a few of their actions, sometimes the regret had more to do with the fact they didn't plan their crime carefully enough to avoid detection. Some "bewailed" that the sentence they received was greater than they anticipated or longer than someone else's who committed a similar crime. Even some were actually moved to tears when expressing these regrets. *But tears do not a contrite person make.* And regret has never been sufficient to prompt a person to change their ways. Neither regret nor even remorse is as meaningful as genuine contrition.

***

Regret is not enough to make people mend their ways.

***

Traditional therapies have always placed a lot of value on people's feelings, and because they are also primarily "talk therapies," they center on what people say. I've seen all too many times how therapists, as well as the victims of irresponsible characters, make the assumption that things are moving in the right direction, because the bad actor shed a tear or two about something horrible he did or said he was sorry. But even when sorrow is genuine, it's not enough. Sorrow is an emotional response usually connected to the loss of something. And while it is always painful to lose, that kind of pain is not, in and of itself, a reliable predictor of change. Individuals who have been in abusive relationships and who give a lot of weight or credence to expressions of regret and sorrow are most often doomed to an escalating level of personal pain and hardship.

True contrition is a rare but essential feature of changing one's life for the better. And while remorse is a prerequisite for contrition, it's still not sufficient for it. Remorse is a genuine empathy-based expression of one's regret over hurting someone else. Psychopaths cannot have it, although they are capable of feigning it. But most people are capable of remorse to some degree—the necessary first step toward contrition. True contrition goes even beyond genuine remorse. The contrite person—their prideful ego crushed and torn asunder by the weight of their guilt and shame—not only hates his or her "sin" but dislikes the person he/she allowed him/herself to become that permitted the travesty to occur in the first place. So, contrition necessarily demands a firm internal resolution, not only to make amends, but also to make of oneself a better person and to conduct oneself in a better fashion in the future. It requires a true *metanoia* or "change of mind." Actually *metanoia* means more than changing your mind, it means to make a 180-degree turn—in other words it means that the person goes in the opposite direction toward a new goal. And even more, it requires work—a lot of the hard, humbling, committed work of character reformation.

Disturbed Characters and Making Amends

It is important for the health of a relationship for the parties to be willing to make amends for injuries inflicted, whether intentionally or inadvertently. But when character disturbance is present in a relationship, the process of making appropriate amends can get quite complicated. Overly conscientious, "neurotic" types in relationships with disturbed or disordered characters can get lured into accepting too much of the responsibility for problems and going the extra mile to try and "fix" them. This approach only further enables the dysfunction in their relationship to continue. And as anyone who's been involved with a disturbed or disordered character knows, how such characters approach the whole idea of acknowledging fault and making amends for damage they've done is as hard to comprehend and accept as it is reflective of the nature of their character dysfunction.

Here is an example. A recently divorced mother is doing her best to raise her already significantly character-impaired teenage son. The mother, who is conscientious, has a lot of guilt and shame resulting from her failed marriage, even for things she had no control over. Her son knows this and uses his mother's feelings of responsibility against her. To get his way he uses manipulation tactics, including minimizing, shaming, and guilt-tripping to skirt responsibility and maintain an abusive upper hand in their relationship. Below is a sample of their typical interaction. (As always, the vignettes depicted in all my writings have been altered in unessential ways to preserve anonymity):

> **Therapist:** What brings you both here today?
>
> **Adolescent:** She (looking glaringly at his mother) thinks I have an attitude problem. But she's always doing stuff that makes me mad. She knows just what to do to piss me off.
>
> **Therapist:** Of course, no one can make you be angry. Beside anger is a normal, healthy emotion, rarely a problem in itself. What is it you do when you're angry?
>
> **Mother:** He curses, says vile, hateful things to me.
>
> **Adolescent:** She starts it. And look, this whole thing is because I shoved her once and not hard and only because she got in my face again. I've told her a million times about that.
>
> **Therapist:** Are you telling me you've been physically aggressive with your mother?
>
> **Adolescent:** I barely touched her. But she wouldn't leave me alone. I kept telling her to back off but she wouldn't. She knows how to get me upset. She never has anything good to say about me. She's constantly on my back—on my case all the time.

Mother: Perhaps he has a point. I do gripe at him sometimes. He's always getting in trouble. I try to help him learn. Maybe I'm too critical, so maybe it's my fault.

The dysfunction in this case is relatively easy to see. One party is overly willing to take responsibility; and the other minimizes, blames, heaps on the guilt, shames, and uses every tactic in the book to resist taking any responsibility while simultaneously manipulating his "opponent" back into her customary one-down position.

The first step I took to restore a proper balance of power in this relationship was to work closely with the person, who at the time I felt was most amenable (i.e., the mother) in an attempt to restore a proper balance of power in the family. And by denying visits to the teenager until I felt he might be sufficiently motivated to work. (At the time, he would have only wanted to come in to attempt to manipulate me and ensure he retained a position of power.) By doing this, I gained therapeutic leverage by defining firmly and adhering to the terms of engagement and set the stage for future work. That work would not merely focus on him surrendering his resistance to accepting responsibility for his actions. Doing that was actually the least demanding thing for him to do. The bigger challenge was developing in him a sufficient sense of obligation to repair the damage he'd done to his mother, his relationship with her, and to his own character development. And how committed he was to the work of making amends would be the best barometer of his progress.

Researchers on character disturbances have long known that a hostile attitude toward accepting obligation is perhaps the single biggest predictor of problematic social behavior. Disturbed characters with narcissistic and antisocial tendencies tend to feel both above the need to accept obligation and disdain for the notion of submitting to what they know are society's expectations of them. Owning shortcomings is distasteful enough for disturbed characters. But making amends involves work, which they don't gravitate toward easily. And it's not just any work that to which they're adverse. They'll expend all kinds of energy in self-serving pursuits. But they simply detest work they perceive is primarily on someone else's behalf, or working for something that's not clearly and intentionally self-serving, despite the potential benefit they might derive in the long run. That's why they tend to give mere assent or "lip service" to the natural demands of a relationship.

"I'm Sorry, but I Still Have to Win."

Disordered characters and most especially disturbed aggressive personalities, tend to view the world as a combat stage. That is one reason it is difficult to benignly confront them. They don't see anything as benign. Benign confrontation is gracious, gentle, without harm. They, however, see most situations as a contest. They have no comprehension of entering into a confrontation without an intent to compete and win at all costs. They expend a lot of mental energy thinking about the battles they want to wage and stances they want to take against the demands of the world. Right from the first minute they think someone is asking something from them, they start planning how they will resist meeting those expectations. They do battle so readily, because they detest the idea of backing down, conceding, or giving ground, even when it would be in their long-term best interest to do so. And therein is the character flaw. They cannot see far enough ahead or with enough objectivity to understand that, in the long run, they might actually win or at least come out ahead.

Habitual combative thinking is what primarily leads to the unnecessarily hostile, confrontational, and defiant attitudes that underlie antisocial conduct. The undisciplined, destructive fighters among us are who they are, because of how they think about life and the world around them. Determined to win at all costs and finding no value in concession, they end up resisting the many efforts of their parents, other authority figures, and society to socialize (i.e., civilize) them.

One way to deal with this combative mindset is to be constantly on the lookout for win-win scenarios. Because they see life as a contest and they always have winning on their minds, finding a way to give disturbed characters some of what they want as a fair exchange for securing something you want can be a helpful strategy and makes living or dealing with them a lot easier. It should be said, however, that no aggressive personality has ever matured into a more pro-social being, until they have dealt directly with their abhorrence of submission of any kind and overcome their penchant for thinking too combatively. At some point they have to accede to the notion that winning in the long run sometimes means conceding or giving ground in the short run. Because to internalize one of society's prohibitions is necessarily an act of submission, they have to learn to be more at peace with the notion that caving-in sometimes is not the end of the world.

"I'm Sorry, but I Still Have to Control Others."

Some disturbed aggressive personalities simply love to build themselves up at the expense of others. It makes them feel powerful to wield almost tyrannical influence over those they perceive as weaker or inferior. They derive pleasure from watching others cower, grovel, or struggle in one-down positions. This disturbance goes from those who derive pleasure from having control over others to those sadistic persons who enjoy inflicting pain and suffering on others—the ultimate, evil use of power and control. These people want what they want and are willing to do whatever it takes to get it. And, what distinguishes these aggressive personalities from assertive personalities is that they don't particularly care about whether others get hurt in the process, nor do they take particular heed not to injure others.

All that said, most aggressive personalities do not set out to hurt others. Their objective, pure and simple, is to get what they want and many believe that the best way to get what they want is to control the significant people in their lives.

When I was doing early research in the area of character disturbance, I happened to encounter a president of a small corporation who boasted to me quite frequently that he was aware that if he weren't successful as a ruthless businessman, he would probably have ended up in prison for most of his life. He said that the secret of his success was that he controlled all the people and all the options. He was quite proud of his achievements. He actually thought that because he knew best, other people were grateful for his "guidance." He was well aware of his aggressive predispositions and the ruthless aggressiveness that permeated all of his interpersonal relations. One day I witnessed this man call a female subordinate into his office and begin to berate her in a most vicious fashion. The degree to which he brandished rage had me shaking a bit in my own boots. After he finished berating her, he warned her of dire consequences if she did not accede to his demands and then dismissed her.

As soon as the woman left the room he looked at me and began to smile and chuckle. He expressed that his pre-planned expression of rage was meant to instill fear in the woman and that he was sure she would be more conscientious about doing his bidding because of it. He also expressed disgust for her weakness. His deliberate use of rage, when in fact he seemed in a jovial mood after the fact, made me aware how rage can be used as a manipulation and control tactic and that it doesn't have to arise out of genuine anger or hurt. The long self-aggrandizing speech this man then engaged in with me also let me know the degree to which he was willing to make his sense of his own power and worth dependent upon the degree to which he could make others feel powerless and worthless. This man was extremely adept at spotting fairly conscientious individuals in one-down positions in their lives who needed support and were willing to put up with his bullying behavior. He surrounded himself with these types of folks and relished opportunities to terrorize them.

Traditional theories on personality development have always presumed that disturbed individuals, who need to control and have power over others, have deep-seated feelings of inferiority or their behavior is a reaction to being themselves severely abused or demeaned as children. While it sometimes turns out that such things may be factors, there is no evidence to suggest that all such personalities have such characteristics in their background; although many will lie about it to engender the sympathy of others. Rather, it seems that the majority of these individuals simply consider themselves as superior to those whom they perceive as weak and take particular delight in controlling others.

How Do I Know He's Really Sorry?

Have you ever asked: How do I know *he's* really sorry? Or maybe your question is: How do I know *she's* really sorry? I get this a lot. One of the more reliable outward signs that a change of heart has actually taken place is the willingness and commitment to make amends. That is, the contrite person is not only "sorry" for what he/she has done but is willing to repair the damage inflicted on the lives of others. I've known so many irresponsible characters who will challenge their understandably hesitant victims with retorts like: "I've said I'm sorry a million times. Now, what else do you want from me?!" —attempting all the while to throw the other party on the defensive for doubting their sincerity. And in proper cognitive-behavioral therapy, where the principal focus is on behavior and encouraging attitudinal and behavioral change, the therapist is much less interested in what a person has to say and much more concerned about what he/she is doing to truly make amends and correct problematic behavior patterns. Talk, as they say, is cheap.

***

A change of heart involves the willingness and commitment to make amends.

***

It's one thing to say you're sorry. But it's quite another to prove it by how hard you work to change. Behavior is the best indicator that real change is taking place. Living and dealing with persons of deficient character is always difficult, but many people increase the level of pain they experience in their relationships with problem characters by buying into the notion that if a person says they're sorry, sheds a tear, or looks unhappy, and appears to mean well, things will necessarily be different. They give too much regard to a person's regret and sorrow and don't look hard enough for evidence of true contrition.

Traditionally-oriented therapists make this same mistake when counseling impaired characters and their relationship partners. A person's genuine willingness and commitment to make amends is always accompanied by plan of action to accomplish precisely those ends. In short, a person's actions always speak louder than their words or even their emotional expressions. The contrite person starts doing things differently. They might not do so perfectly or every time. But they make a constant effort at reforming their conduct, and when they fall short they admit it and do their best to get back on course. So, therapy that just focuses on getting someone to express their feelings or communicate their regrets is likely doomed to be ineffective in fostering meaningful change.

***

Behavior is the best indicator of real change.

***

I simply cannot count the number of times during my professional career when people, who have done something horrible, feel badly about it in some way afterwards. Often, they felt badly every time they repeated the same behavior. Having some regret simply isn't enough to make a person mend their ways. I also can't count the times that those affected by another's misdeeds were so swayed by the wrongdoer's display of tears or a claim of regret that they unfortunately helped "enable" that person to avoid real change. Therapists can be unduly swayed by such displays as well. Sentiment never stripped anyone of their character defects. It takes a lot of concerted effort to overcome our shortcomings. The truly contrite individual works to make amends, to do better, and above all, to be better. That always involves demonstrable, consistent behavior—behavior that can be observed, monitored, encouraged, rewarded, and measured in sound cognitive-behavioral therapy.

How Real Contrition Looks

Having some regret simply isn't enough to make a person mend their ways; and important lessons can be gleaned by distinguishing between selfish, personal regret and genuine repentance. All too often, we see on the news sagas involving a public official, not only caught in scandalous behavior but also exposed for all the numerous and colorful lies he told to keep from being outed. Much of the truth about the behavior itself has finally come to light, and as a result, the once brazenly feisty official—some of whom have the audacity to attack the reporters' questions as a tactic to keep them on the defensive—appeared to be eating some humble pie as he proclaimed his "acceptance of responsibility" and "regret" for all those he had harmed before the cameras. We should always expect new versions of this story, with new actors, and unfortunately, new levels of preposterousness each time the tale is told. Nonetheless, there are important lessons that can be gleaned from distinguishing between selfish, personal regret and genuine repentance.

A deficient capacity for true empathy and contrition is one of the hallmarks of the impaired character. And for some character types, this deficiency can be extreme. There is a big difference between regretting the consequences to oneself of bad behavior (e.g., getting caught, paying fines, receiving other social sanctions) and experiencing genuine empathy-based remorse for the injury caused to others. For a person to experience any degree of genuine contrition, which could prompt them to change their ways, two things must occur.

1. They not only have to feel genuinely badly about what they have done (i.e., guilty), but

2. they must also be internally unnerved about the kind of person they must have allowed themselves to become (i.e., shameful) to have behaved so irresponsibly. Their shame and guilt must then propel them to make of themselves a better person.

In the case of Sam and Audrey, what would true contrition look like? Both have some serious issues. Sam needs to give up thinking that violence will solve the problem. Audrey needs to confront her irresponsible spending. Both need to recognize that each has room for improvement and that they need a plan of action. When both put the plan into action and have their *Aha!* moments, then we can say that they are contrite.

For the mother and her troubled son, how would a contrite son look? He would give his mother due respect and begin to take appropriate responsibility for his own behavior, perhaps by doing some household chores on a regular basis. Contrition requires repentance, a word that means, "turning around and going in the opposite direction." Contrition means that one will travel a different relational path.

Obviously, these cases are much more complex and the answers too easy, but the point is that when someone is contrite, they behave differently over an extended period of time, not until the next time they are provoked. How do you know that sorry means that "I won't do it again," when there is real, lasting change? This means that, frankly, you're not going to know immediately; because change takes time. And true, if your situation is bad enough, you may not be able or willing to wait. That is why, benign confrontation works best when problems first appear, before the cycle of bad behavior has escalated.

A Word about Shame and Guilt

Because an immature or impaired conscience is a hallmark feature of the disturbed character, such characters have a diminished capacity to experience genuine guilt over actions or intended actions that injure others. So when they're thinking about doing something, disordered characters rarely think about how their actions might affect others or possibly transgress ethical or moral boundaries. To the degree that they might have at least some rudimentary conscience, they're able to quickly and effectively block out thoughts of right and wrong, when they're seriously contemplating how to get something they want. Not caring enough about how their behavior might impact someone else, they simply give the rightness or wrongness of their plans no serious consideration. They might very well know that others would view their behavior as wrong, but they can still make excuses and "justify" their wrongful acts with ease. Over time, this guiltless way of thinking promotes a pervasive attitude of irresponsibility.

Disordered characters also have a deficient sense of shame. They almost never think of how some action of theirs might negatively reflect the kind of person they are. This is such an important point, because it could easily be said that a key feature of the most disordered individuals is that they neither care enough nor think enough about how their patterns of behavior reflect on their character. What's more, when disturbed characters do perceive that someone is judging them in a negative manner, they easily think that it's the other person who has the problem. Some of the most severely disturbed characters might even count it as a badge of honor that they are not affected by the opinions of others and hold onto their grandiose and unrealistic self-images, despite a track record of wreaking havoc in the lives of those they work or live with. Over time, their shameless thinking fosters the development of quite a brazen attitude.

Guilt is the bad feeling most of us have when we think we've done something wrong. Shame is all about our feelings about ourselves as persons of worth. People who feel shame often report feeling "dirty" or "stained" in some way. When our patterns of behavior habitually cause problems and pain for others, most of us reflect upon or think about those behaviors with a sense of both shame and guilt. We feel bad for doing wrong and strive not to do similar things again. And, we feel ashamed of ourselves and vow to be better persons. Disturbed and disordered characters don't engage in this kind of thinking. Lacking an appropriate sense of guilt, and without a sufficient sense of shame, they don't engage in the same kind of reflective thinking that enables most of us to grow, change, and improve ourselves.

While I have known thousands of repeat offenders over the years who felt badly each and every time they misbehaved, I've never known anyone who really turned their lives around just because they felt guilty. Regret and remorse weren't enough to make them change either. Rather, it was only when they could no longer live with themselves and the kind of person they'd allowed themselves to become that things finally turned around. Shame saved them when guilt, regret, and remorse all failed. It prompted them to undertake the arduous task of forging a better character.

Take Away

True contrition occurs when the person can no longer live with themselves and becomes invested in making of themselves a better person. It can't just be an "acceptance of responsibility" spoken on the lips accompanied by a steadfast refusal to pay the price (and not merely the price of public embarrassment) of duly earned consequences. It can't just be crocodile tears of remorse openly displayed but that aren't accompanied by a change of one's style. It can't be the mere broadcasting of regret that's not paired with clear action to make amends. True contrition involves a change of direction and then acting differently. It's humbly reckoning with oneself, the deficiencies in one's character that allowed the person to indulge in the misbehavior in the first place, coupled with a firm commitment to exorcise those character defects so that the errors are not repeated.

Empowerment Tools

Having some regret isn't enough to make a person mend their ways, and being swayed by the wrongdoer's display of tears or claims of regret helps enable that person to avoid real change.

1. The evidence for change in a relationship is only different behavior.

2. Change takes time, which doesn't happen immediately. If, however, your situation is bad enough and you are at risk, you may not be able or willing to wait. That is why, benign confrontation works best when problems first appear, before the cycle of bad behavior escalates and gets out of control.

Chapter Six
Truth, Lies, and Manipulation

The Power of Truth

A most important factor in promoting wellness is honesty. If healthy confrontation is going to be effective or ever have a chance, it must be rooted in truth. However, as we all know, human beings have an incredible capacity to lie. This includes the ability to deceive ourselves as well as others. Recognizing that fact and committing to being truly honest in our dealings with others as well as ourselves is key, not only to our emotional health but also to the integrity of our character.

While we uphold truth as imperative, we're never obliged to say things that might conceal other important details. This is a major manipulation tactic. And we don't use the truth as a weapon to needlessly hurt another person. For example, we don't have to tell someone how hideous we think they look in a particular outfit. Nor is it appropriate to broadcast every unseemly thing we know about someone else. But if we're to forge a character of integrity, it's crucial that when it really counts, especially within the context of a relationship, we don't con or manipulate others, and we don't lie to ourselves.

Lies are always near the heart of a
disturbed character's trouble.

***

Whether I'm dealing with character-impaired individuals or others, I'm always on the lookout for the lies that are near the heart of a person's trouble and for tactful but direct ways to confront those lies. The "evil" that invades a person's life is almost always vested in a lie, and it's no accident that philosophers, religious sages, and other writers who personify pure evil (i.e., the devil) rightly cast the creature as the "Father of Lies." My experience has taught me not only that evil exists but also that a lie is often its closest companion. And in my work over the years, I've found that it's impossible to truly deal with evil without confronting the lies that so frequently spawn it.

Character-impaired folks have particular problems with honesty. Most of the time, they're aware of their dishonesty and consciously and deliberately seek to deceive others for the purposes of exploitation and control. But to the degree they are neurotic, they also deceive themselves about what they're doing. Sometimes, they can be so habitual in their self-deceptions and get so comfortable with the lies they tell themselves that they actually begin to believe those lies. But to the degree they're simply character-deficient as opposed to neurotic, the less they need self-deception and the more they are concerned with conning others.

The Truth about Pathological Lying

Some of the most seriously disturbed and disordered characters lie so habitually and so casually (and often, seemingly unnecessarily), that we often speak of such lying as "pathological," because of how irrational it can be. But as illogical as their lying might seem, most disturbed characters have a rational purpose in lying, namely to maintain a position of advantage over others.

**Disturbed characters have a rational purpose in
lying — to maintain a position of advantage.**

Neurotic people, on the other hand, owe many of their unresolved emotional conflicts to the self-deceptions they engage in unconsciously. Sometimes things happen to us that hurt and sometimes we make mistakes that cause us pain. But when, out of fear or pride, we deny or repress instead of acknowledge and deal with the various things behind our pain, we inevitably create even more trouble for ourselves. In a fundamental way, all of our neurotic "defenses" are really deceptions. And at the heart of traditional therapy for neurotics is setting an atmosphere in which it feels safe to honestly self-reckon. A good therapist's first duty is to prove him/herself trustworthy and accepting, which allows the necessary helping relationship develop. But the client's primary burden is to muster the courage and commitment to honestly reflect upon and deal with their issues. In so doing, they truly promote their own healing.

But when dealing with character-impaired people, lies must always be confronted directly, albeit tactfully. Then the character-impaired person must be "invited" to try out a more adaptive, alternative behavior. In other words, they have to be taught to seek what they want in less underhanded, destructive ways. Of course they have to learn a lot more than that, too, but the main point here is that absolutely nothing can be accomplished without them demonstrating the willingness to stop deceiving, conning, manipulating, and trying to manage impressions.

So here's the tried and true axiom that years of experience have validated: Honesty has power. Truth has the power to set the neurotic soul free, and it has the power to expose the "evil" in the character-impaired person's typical *modus operandi*. It's also a trust and respect builder. Still, dealing truthfully with issues in a manner that's courageous and firm, yet devoid of all malice and unnecessary judgment, is a most rare and difficult skill to hone. But that, as Eric Fromm might say, is the art in loving.

Lying: The Ultimate Manipulation Tactic

But disordered characters do not make it easy. Lying helps keep them one-up on you and a step ahead of you. It is, by far, the most effective manipulation and responsibility-avoidance behavior. Disordered characters not only lie frequently, but they sometimes lie even when there appears no obvious or useful purpose for the lying. They are also expert at lying in a wide variety of ways, some of which are quite subtle.

For the disordered character, lying serves many purposes. But mainly, lying serves to give a manipulator an advantage over someone else. Disordered characters don't want you to know what they're all about or what they're up to. That would level the playing field in your encounters with them. They want to keep you in the dark and keep you guessing. One of the best ways to do this is by deception.

There are so many ways to lie that it's almost impossible to list them all. But disordered characters are knowledgeable about even the most subtle and stealthy ways to lie and are artful in their use of the various forms of lying.

Lies of Omission

One subtle approach to lying is lying by omission. When someone wants to pull the wool over your eyes, they don't have to make an obviously absurd or bogus claim. Many times, all they have to do is make sure they don't tell the whole truth about something. It's as simple as leaving out a very important detail or something crucial to understanding the whole picture. Here is an example: an aging manager is concerned about his job security, because the company has just been sold. He asks his boss if there are plans to lay off any employees, including, of course, him. His boss tells him flatly that there are no such plans. But he doesn't tell him that he is going to get a new, younger assistant, who will replace him in the next few months. Sometimes, what a person doesn't say or do can be a much more effective manipulation tool.

Vagueness

Another type of subtle lying is the use of vagueness. When you confront a disturbed character about an issue, they may give you an answer; but they might also be so vague about the details that you end up remaining largely in the dark. Sometimes, the disordered character can manipulate you effectively by doing just the opposite—by using specificity in a response in such a way that it may provide a limited answer to the question you've asked, but without providing additional detail that would better address the intent of your question.

Distortion

Lying by distortion of crucial details provides one other way to obscure the bigger picture and mislead someone. In fact, when someone really wants to lie effectively, they'll often recite a litany of true facts (all to give the impression that they're on a truth-telling spree) while simultaneously leaving out a crucial detail or two or distorting the true nature of an important fact.

Lying is such a habit for disordered characters that sometimes they end up halfway believing their lies. That's true not only for the lies they tell others but for the lies they tell themselves. By lying so often about the reality of situations, the disturbed character obstructs and resists any chance that they will internalize the most essential principles of responsible conduct. Sometimes the web of lies gets so convoluted that they can't distinguish the lies from the truth.

While lying is to make an untrue statement with an intent to deceive, there are other ways to create a false or misleading impression in order to distort the truth, including rationalization, minimization, and blaming.

Making Excuses: Rationalization

Making excuses, or rationalization, is a way to avoid and then justifying reasons for not telling the truth. This can be an effective manipulation tactic, because the person can deny the reality of the truth and explain why he didn't tell you in the first place, all the while justifying himself to you and perhaps to himself as well. Because effective manipulation tactics simultaneously put others on the defensive, while obscuring or denying the malevolent intent of the person using them. Truth is like the light of day and disturbed people prefer that you stay in the dark. Such tactics are particularly effective on neurotic individuals—especially those of us who always want to think the best of people and who strive hard to understand what would make a person behave in a problematic way.

Some of the tactics disturbed characters use to avoid responsibility and manipulate others have been traditionally viewed as ego defense mechanisms, arising out of the erroneous, but a still common notion, that everyone feels badly to some degree when they want act on their primal urges and against the interest of the greater good. As a result, it was presumed that everyone exhibiting such behaviors was defending against feelings of shame and guilt. But, as I have pointed out before, all metaphors can be stretched beyond their capacity to be useful, and traditional metaphors about why people do the things they do become greatly strained when trying to understand and deal with disordered characters.

The concept of defense mechanisms becomes the most greatly tested when we're trying to truly understand the behavioral habits and tactics of the disordered character. When it comes to understanding and dealing with the disturbed character, many of the behaviors we have traditionally thought of as defense mechanisms are better viewed as automatic (although conscious and deliberate) behaviors that simultaneously serve to justify or excuse antisocial behavior, obstruct the internalization of pro-social values (avoid responsibility), effectively manipulate and control others who don't quite understand the true intentions and motivations of the disordered character, and manage the impressions others have so as to keep any social pressure to change and tell the truth at bay. The manipulation and responsibility avoidance tactics disordered characters employ are too numerous to list. In fact, almost any behavior can and has been used at one time or another by a disturbed character as a means to avoid responsibility and manipulate others. In the end, by frequently engaging in these behaviors disturbed characters reinforce in their own minds the notion that their preferred way of doing things is okay, and there is no need to change their ways of relating to others.

Sometimes the disordered character will go to great lengths to attempt to justify a behavior he knows is wrong or knows others regard as wrong. Disturbed characters are forever making excuses and lying about their harmful or hurtful conduct. They have an answer for everything they're challenged about. When others confront them, they come up with a litany of reasons why their behavior was justified. In my work with disordered characters, I've heard literally thousands of excuses for irresponsible behavior.

The traditional thinking on rationalization, of course, is that it is an unconscious defense mechanism. The theory behind this is that a person unknowingly tries to alleviate pangs of guilt by finding some way to grant legitimacy to their behavior. But if someone really is feeling pangs of guilt, the uneasiness they feel about their behavior is internal. So, when rationalization as a defense mechanism is truly employed, the exculpating dialogue that takes place is internal. When disturbed characters use the responsibility-avoidance tactic of rationalization (alternately: justification or excuse-making), they're not primarily trying to reconcile their conduct with their consciences, but rather trying to manipulate others into getting off their case by getting them to "buy into" the excuses they make. Their rationalizations are part of an external dialogue designed to cast the disturbed character as not as bad a person as others might otherwise think he is. So, their excuses are also part of their impression management scheme. Habitually attempting to justify behaviors they know are regarded by most people as clearly wrong is also another way the disturbed character resists internalizing appropriate standards of conduct and controls and therefore makes it ever more likely he will engage in the wrongful behavior again.

The responsibility-avoidance behaviors are effective manipulation tools, because when used effectively by the disordered character, they simultaneously put others on the defensive, while obscuring or denying the malevolent intent of the person using the tactic. The tactics are particularly effective on neurotic individuals, especially those who always want to think the best of people and who strive hard to understand what would make a person behave in a problematic way.

It is extremely important to understand the mode of behavior (i.e., the mindset and emotional state) the disordered character is in when he is in the process of lying. He is not in the defensive mode. It may appear so, especially to someone who has been indoctrinated with traditional notions about the motivations of behavior, and especially when some of the tactics can prompt a good neurotic, who is confronting negative behavior to feel like an attacker. But at the very moment the disturbed character is making excuses (rationalizing), blaming others (scapegoating), lying, etc., he is fighting.

When you confront a disordered character about a harmful behavior, he is more than likely fully aware of the pro-social principle at stake. For example, when you point out that he was wrong to strike his wife and then lie about it, he understands very well that society frowns this kind of behavior. So, when he starts with the tactics and rationalizing his behavior, he is well aware that society wants him to accept and submit to the principle that it's not okay to strike your spouse. He's also aware how civilized persons view the kind of people who, despite society's rules, engage in such behavior. But he's still actively resisting submission to this principle and fighting against internalizing the value. He also doesn't want you on his case or to see him as the uncivilized sort that he is. He wants you to back off, accept his justifications, and keep the kind of image of him he wants you to have. So, whenever a disturbed character uses these tactics, you know one thing absolutely for certain: he will do it again. He'll do it again, because the use of the tactic testifies to the fact that he's still at war with the principle. He's fighting the very socialization process that could civilize him. You could say that he's defending his ego, but that would be a relatively insignificant point and a distortion of the bigger picture. The main thing to remember is that when he engages in these behaviors, he is primarily fighting submission to the principles that serve the greater good and simultaneously trying to manipulate you into seeing things his way.

Minimization: Trivializing Behavior as a Manipulation Tactic

Minimization is a way to avoid the impact of the whole truth, making it seem less than, less important than it is. When he uses a tactic of minimizing a lie, for example, "It didn't hurt that bad," the disturbed character is attempting to convince someone else that the wrongful thing he did wasn't really as bad or as harmful as he knows it was and as he knows the other person thinks it was.

On the other hand, when neurotics do something they think might negatively impact another, they tend to "catastrophize" the situation or become overly concerned with the damage they might have done. Conversely, disturbed characters are overly prone to minimizing the seriousness of their misconduct and trivializing the damage they cause in their relationships and to the general social order.

Minimization is a close cousin to the tactic of denial, which is also often misinterpreted as a defense mechanism. When he uses the tactic of minimization, he might admit part of what he did was wrong, and usually not the most serious part. By using the tactic, he tries to manipulate others into thinking that he's not such bad a person (impression management) and continues his active war against submission to a principle of social behavior.

As is true when other tactics are used, when the disordered character minimizes the nature and seriousness of his conduct, you know for sure that he is likely to engage in the same or similar behaviors again. As long as he continues to minimize, he won't take seriously the problems he needs to correct. It isn't that he doesn't recognize the seriousness of the issues. If he didn't think others regarded the issue as serious, he wouldn't feel the need to trivialize it. But refusing to accept the principle at hand and to accept the need to change his stance indicate he's sure to repeat his misconduct. People use these tactics for a lot of reasons, but the biggest reason is that they generally work for them.

***

People use the tactics that work for them.

***

I remember one of the first times I witnessed the effectiveness of the minimization tactic. A couple had come to my office for counseling, and the woman's main complaint was that she was becoming increasingly fearful of what appeared to be her husband's escalating level of aggressiveness. She complained that during an argument, he shoved her, and, because he'd never done that before, it concerned her. His comment: "Yeah, I might have touched her and pushed her a little bit, but you could hardly call it a 'shove' and there's no way she can claim I hurt her or meant to hurt her. She's making me out to be a monster, and I'm not. Besides, she pushed me to the brink!" This man's statement combined several effective tactics from minimizing and trivializing the event ("touched her and pushed her a little bit") to denial of malevolent intent ("no way she can claim I meant to hurt her"), vilifying the victim ("She's making me out to be a monster") and externalizing the blame ("She pushed me to the brink!") among others. Before long, the woman was back-peddling and feeling bad for even bringing up the issue. Their true situation was buried under a barrage of half-truths, false claims, and discrediting remarks, all designed to portray himself in the best light possible. These tactics worked for him and she acquiesced.

In my work with this couple, it also became clear how traditional notions about human behavior—especially paradigms designed to understand neurosis—are inadequate and sometimes even destructive, when it comes to understanding the *modus operandi* of the disturbed character. Having been a veteran of traditional therapy, the woman in this case commented many times that she knew she was "making him [her husband] defensive," and she that didn't want to make him feel badly about himself, but she didn't know how else to address the issue. Clearly, she perceived him to be in a "defensive" posture, when he was in fact on the offensive. What was even more disconcerting was the look of resignation on her face as she herself assumed the submissive position after his barrage of tactics succeeded in their intent. Later in therapy when she started to be assertive and confront her husband, he didn't know what to do at first. Then he resorted to his old tactics once again. It took him a long time to figure out that she wasn't buying his lies any more.

Playing the Blame Game as a Manipulation Tactic

By habitually blaming others for their own indiscretions, disturbed characters try to shift the burden of telling the whole truth, while resisting change of their problematic attitudes and behavior patterns.

Perhaps no behavior that disordered characters are prone to displaying is more common than their tendency to blame others when they do something wrong. Confront them on something they did that was insensitive, inappropriate, hurtful, or even harmful, and you'll find them playing the blame game—pinning the fault on someone or something else. You'll often hear them claim that some person or circumstance made them do what they did, instead of acknowledging that they had a choice about how to respond to the situation and failed to choose wisely.

The tactic of blaming has sometimes been called projecting the blame. The term projection stems from psychodynamic psychology and refers to one of the automatic mental behaviors conceptualized by traditional theorists as ego defense mechanisms. The rationale behind that notion is that sometimes individuals unconsciously "project" onto others motivations, intentions, or actions that they actually harbor themselves but which they would feel far too unnerved or guilty about to acknowledge as their own.

***

**Disordered characters know what they are doing
and that it's wrong.**

***

Neurotic individuals do indeed unknowingly engage in projection defenses. But disordered characters know what they are doing. They are fully conscious about what they know others would see as the wrongfulness of their behavior, despite the fact that they might be perfectly comfortable with their course of action themselves. They don't have enough guilt or shame about what they're doing to change course. Nor are they so consumed with emotional pain that they must ascribe to others the motivations they can't tolerate in themselves. Rather, when they blame others for their wrongful acts, it's simply an attempt to justify their stance by casting themselves as being in a position where they simply had no choice but to respond the way they did. In this way, they simultaneously evade responsibility as well as manipulate and manage the impressions of others. The tactic goes hand in hand with the tactic of portraying oneself as a victim. It's typically an effective tactic that gets others to pay attention to everyone or everything else except the disordered character and his wrongful behavior as the source of a problem.

Sometimes the tactic of blaming can be quite subtle. By calling attention to a wide variety of contributing circumstances, a manipulator can effectively obscure his or her role in the creation of a problem. This "It wasn't me" tactic is hard to detect when your attention is drawn to other "culprits" through this diversionary sleight-of-hand.

Holding manipulators and other disturbed characters accountable for their choices and actions is a must. Without confrontation, a person who won't acknowledge his or her bad choices and bad habits and repeatedly blames others for his shortcomings will never correct his erroneous thinking or behavior. Whenever he plays the blame game, you know the disturbed character has no intentions of changing his ways. Habitually blaming others for his own indiscretions is a major way the disturbed character resists modifying his problematic attitudes and behavior patterns.

Confessions of a Sincere Heart

When people start telling the truth amazing things can happen and change is possible. Like many, I've been quite touched by the heartwarming story of Ted Williams. Ted "Golden Voice" Williams had a God-given talent and a budding career until he lost himself, his family, and fortune to a life on the streets from chronic substance abuse. But he found new hope. Videos of Ted Williams panhandling on the streets and giving passers-by a sample of his meant-for-the-media voice went viral after being posted on YouTube in January, 2011. As a result, he was re-discovered and offered some amazing opportunities to put his talent to good use and rebuild his life. What touched me more than the particulars of his story, however, was his sincere and ardent testimony about the factors he believes are responsible for life-changing circumstances.

I've listened to and read enough of the interviews this man has given to get a fairly good idea about what he believes saved him from a life of faded glory, broken dreams, and despair. He has been adamant with everyone he has talked to, and his message appears clear, truthful, and soul-baring. And his message resonates with thousands of similar stories that I've come across in my work with individuals who struggled with character issues but eventually managed to make the commitment necessary to forge a better sense of self.

One of the most remarkable things to me about Mr. Williams's story is the reaction some of the interviewers when they hear his testimony. Naturally, all were impressed with his incredible talent and joyful about the fact that he was no longer on the streets. He knew that he had a God-given talent and that he took it for granted and defaulted on the values instilled in him for the sake of a quick high. He credited a higher power for saving him from the brink of despair and bestowing abundant blessings upon him as he strove to rebuild his life. He pointed to his sense of shame for what he had let himself become before finding the strength to turn things around. In so doing, he echoed the testimony of thousands of once-struggling characters who eventually found the keys to change their lives for the better.

But many of his assertions, as profound as they are, weren't "politically correct." From his admission that character deficiencies led him down the path that eventually resulted in addiction, to his insistence that a profound sense of shame finally led him to finally stand up for the values his mother tried to instill in him. (Mental health professionals still generally consider shame a toxic commodity as opposed to a potentially powerful positive motivator.) He definitely cut against the grain with respect to popular thinking about how people get themselves into trouble and what they need to do to get themselves out of it.

Ted has been an inspiration. He, like many others, made changes in their lives by taking a hard look at his life. Even though relapse is always a possibility, Ted knows the truth of his ordeal and he encourages others to be truthful about their situation as well. Health can only begin when we acknowledge the truth. Without it, we cannot stay the course. Without it, we don't see the value of the opportunities and support when they come our way. A truthful person is humble about his gifts and is aware of his obligations and responsibilities.

Take Away

Committing ourselves to being truly honest in our dealings with others as well as ourselves is key, not only to our emotional health but also to the integrity of our character. Lies are always near the heart of a person's troubled relationships. Holding manipulators and other disturbed characters accountable to tell the truth is a must. Without confrontation, a person who won't acknowledge his or her bad choices and bad habits and repeatedly blames others for his shortcomings will never correct his erroneous thinking or behavior.

Empowerment Tools

1. There is power in honesty.

2. Lies are manipulations of the truth and they come in many forms: lies of omission, vagueness, and distortion.

3. Some tactics that disturbed people use to manipulate people into believing these lies include: lying, making excuses (rationalization), minimization, and blaming.

Chapter Seven
The Real Face of Change

So far in this book, we have said that there is hope, but often the best chance for a satisfying relationship and the necessary change that has to happen, comes from practicing the art of healthy confrontation. We then discussed some of the obstacles that you can encounter, including the personality of the person you need to confront. If that person has a disturbed or underdeveloped character, there are specific things to watch out for and anticipate before you confront him or her. The troubled people that you may love and live with have certain predilections and behaviors that must be factored into account before you plan any healthy confrontation. You might also have internal issues and behaviors you have to deal with as well. You may wonder how your relationship has ended up a wreak, but after you've come to the realization that something has to change and you are sufficiently prepared to act assertively, you also have to have an idea what your success will look like, what you are aiming for, what health looks like in your relationship. In other words, how will you know that the person is contrite and willing to change, and how can you trust that person, whether disturbed or not, to tell you the truth? This chapter continues the theme of what change looks like and how you can know when it really happens.

Can People Change Their Personality?

Research has been mounting for some time that the concept of "personality" is not as well-defined as we have long tended to think.

(See Appendix for the definition of "personality.") The evidence also suggests that the patterns of behavior that define our personality are not nearly as stable or as immutable as many still believe.

That all of us have a unique personality is generally believed without dispute. And by the currently accepted definition, our personalities are comprised of traits we innately possess, the ways we've learned to cope, and the habits of relating we've developed as a result of both of these factors. Our acquired habits prompt us to behave in some fairly predictable ways in a wide variety of situations, which is pretty much what defines our core personality "style."

Sometimes our habitual ways of seeing and doing things (i.e., our personalities) can be a source of trouble for us and others. This is the definition of a personality or character disturbance or disorder. And, as I have asserted many times, for a variety of sociocultural reasons, character dysfunction has become the most dominant mental and behavioral health issue of our time. But many folks have their doubts about whether it's even possible to do something about the problem. They wonder: Can we really change who we are? Because if we can't, why bother about confronting another person in order to get them to change?

There are many misconceptions about personality, character, and the nature of personality or character disturbances. Some believe our personality is strictly a product of our innate, biologically-based traits and predispositions, perhaps even in our genes. And others believe that even when someone makes outward changes in their behavior, it's simply not possible for them to change the person they are "inside." This is the notion that "it's impossible for a leopard to change its spots." If you hold these notions, it is likely that you'll believe personality is simply not something you can modify. Abundant research, however, has been telling us something much different.

Several factors contribute to how much our personalities might change over our lifetimes. Time and the wisdom that often comes with it, are two of those factors. How many people think the same way, hold the same values, look at the world the same way, or even perceive ourselves at age fifty as they did when they were teens? It seems the more we come to know about what is around us and the more we come to understand ourselves, the more likely our opinions and attitudes about a whole host of things are going to change. We might even look back differently on the person we were twenty or so years ago. For example, we might reflect on the tattoo that's still on our hip or recall the person we once thought hung the moon is just a total creep. And say to ourselves, "What in the blazes was I thinking?!" That's when we realize that over time, we actually have changed, both in our attitudes and in our behavior. So we're really not the same, even though to some degree we think of ourselves as the same person that we have always been at the core. There is nothing more telling that going back to a high school reunion and seeing all the cool guys with big bellies and no hair or the hot girls with wrinkles and dyed blond hair. And that's just outward appearances; inside we hope that we're all more loving and caring than we were then. That is part of what it means to be a mature individual—that you put away your childhood and accept adult responsibilities to care for yourself, others, and the world. Without change there can be no growing up.

***

Personalities can change over time and hopefully they do.

***

Perhaps the greatest variable affecting our ability and/or willingness to change our personality is the degree of comfort we have with ourselves as a person. Some of us have liked the person we have been from early on and see absolutely no reason to change anything about ourselves. Others have not only been "set in their ways" for a long time but have also grown increasingly and more stubbornly fixed in those ways as time progressed. So the question always to be asked is: Are we so content with ourselves as we are that we simply have no motivation to change? Or perhaps an easier question might be: Are our loved ones so content with who we are that they don't see any way we can be better people? And it will come as no surprise that one thing that distinguishes the more seriously disturbed characters from their relatively neurotic counterparts is how content they tend to be with the kind of person they are, despite all the problems their way of doing things cause.

Dozens of people contact me every month who have read my books and see themselves or someone they know as one of the characters depicted in those books. Some see themselves as one of the neurotic personalities I depict. Others see themselves one of the more character-disturbed or disordered types. Most of all them ask the same questions: "Can I change?" and "If so, how do I go about it?" One of things I'm quick to point out to them in my reply is that merely asking such questions, which necessarily indicates the person is feeling some internal pressure to change, is a pretty good indicator that change is indeed possible for them, even though it will inevitably entail some hard work — perhaps even more work than they bargained for.

***

**Thinking you need to change is a good indication
that change is possible for you.**

***

Changing one's "stripes" or "spots" doesn't necessarily require getting professional help. What matters most of all is the desire to change and the willingness to truthfully confront and correct the dysfunctional thinking patterns and behavior patterns causing problems. Still, therapists who specialize in personality disturbances, and therefore have a variety of tools at their disposal to facilitate the process change, can come in quite handy when changing who you are is your agenda. While no one can simply will away their innate or more biologically-based predispositions, any of us can learn to modify the way we look at things and the manner in which we have habitually approached things. Confronting problematic attitudes and changing them, targeting old habits and modifying them, and reinforcing ourselves for every effort is the process by which we can indeed change the kind of person we have been. Sometimes, our biologically-based predispositions are so strong and influential that meaningful change is not possible without medications to assist us (as in the case of Borderline Personality Disorder, where the ability to self-regulate mood is not only impaired but also the cause of many relationship problems.) But with some sound cognitive-behavioral intervention and the help of appropriate medication when necessary, even some of the most dysfunctional personalities can be modified.

***

**We can modify the way we look at and
approach life despite old habits.**

***

Having specialized in the assessment and treatment of personality dysfunction for a long time, I've had to come to terms with the fact that change never comes easily and sometimes doesn't come at all. For a variety of reasons, some personality dysfunctions are simply too severe and too intractable to be modified by any of the means presently available. But over the years I've witnessed many genuine success stories, and I can say without hesitation that there's nothing quite like being a part of someone's personal transformation and character development. But sometimes, the change process requires the "patience of Job." It's not uncommon for a more severely disturbed character to be completely unprepared" (i.e., insufficiently internally motivated) for change at the same point in time that everyone else around them is desperate for things to be different. But that never stopped me, nor should it you, from calling out the issues clearly and directly. And that's why when life's circumstances and a softening of a person's heart finally led them to a greater openness to change, they sought counsel from the person who dared to confront their pathology honestly and who they therefore had come to believe they could trust to guide them.

The Real Face of Change

Change—legitimate, genuine, potentially lasting change—always manifests itself in the behavior of the here-and-now. It's not an empty promise to be better but a here-and-now decision to do differently. And over the years, I've had the blessing and privilege to witness some of the most impaired characters make significant changes in their lives. Unfortunately, I've also encountered many persons extremely resistant to change—even among those who vociferously protested that they were a different person. This begets the question of how you know someone is really making changes, especially when they're involved in the therapeutic process.

***

Genuine, potentially lasting change always manifests itself in the here-and-now.

***

People working toward genuine change have a distinctive character about them and display some readily observable signs that they truly mean business. Folks who are all talk and no action are also easy to spot, especially if you know what to look for. Here's an example based on a real case (with details altered to ensure anonymity). It's a portion of an interview I did with an individual who'd had repeated problems with the law and was facing incarceration for the first time:

Q: Why are you here today?

A: They told me if I get some counseling I'll have a better shot at getting some justice.

Q: And who is "they?"

A: My lawyer.

Q: Okay. So, in what way do you think I might be able to help you?

A: To tell you the truth, I don't really need no help. I seen someone before. Lots of times. Didn't do no good, though. But I got my act together now. I ain't gonna do those things that got me in so much trouble no more.

Q: You've had therapy before?

A: Yeah, I seen lots of doctors and everything, and my momma..., she put me in one of those places one time and the judge said they was gonna help me get over what they said was my depression and stuff.

Q: Were you depressed?

A: I was when I got there!

Q: What had you done that your mom and the judge thought you needed that kind of treatment?

A: Man, they was makin' it out like I was some kind of criminal or something. I had missed a little school, but I was going to get me a job. And they got me for havin' some "weed" in my car, but I wasn't gonna sell it like they said, and besides, who doesn't sell a little weed or get a little high sometimes.

Q: Were there other problems?

A: Well, my momma says I pushed her down, but I didn't really, she tripped. And she was in my face, just like she does a lot. I told her to back off but she wouldn't. And they're calling it assault and battery. But I'm tellin' you, I'm a changed man now. I even go to church sometimes and everything. All this other stuff they're saying about me is just bull^&*&^!

Q: If I were to decide to work with you, you'd have to show me some degree of willingness to really change.

A: But I am changed. I already done told you that.

Q: Saying you've changed is one thing. Showing that it's true is quite another. And in just the few minutes you've been with me, whenever you had the opportunity to accept responsibility, instead you *minimized* the seriousness and criminality of your misbehavior, you *rationalized* and *made excuses*, and you *blamed others* for your situation. And you made no attempt to stop yourself. Instead, you did the very same things right here today that you've done for a long time and that got you to the point of facing the consequences you're now facing. So, from my standpoint, I'm not seeing that you have actually done much changing or that you've even given much attention to the task. And if I were to take you on as a patient, my job would be to encourage and reward you for doing things very differently. Your job would be to catch and correct yourself whenever you're tempted to engage in any of the tactics you typically try and which I have outlined on this thinking errors and manipulation tactics worksheet right here. And you can start by admitting that talk is cheap and that you haven't really done all that much to change your ways of doing things.

A: I guess ya got me there, doc. What's next?

***

This example only illustrates a start for a potentially helpful therapeutic process. And suffice it to say that not all my encounters with disturbed characters have been anywhere near as promising as this one was at the start. Besides, even this case proved to be a very much up and down, backward and forward situation for quite some time. But I provide the example to help illustrate two things.

1. If you want to tell if someone is really intent on changing or if change is actually happening, look for what you experience and how they act in the here-and-now.

2. Any therapeutic encounter with a disturbed character will be quite different.

The most important thing to remember is that what a person says or intends is not the best indicator of change, rather it's always about their *behavior*. Because behavior demonstrates their capitulation to the values and principles we expect people to uphold in our society. And once you see specific behaviors, you'll get a clearer picture in the here and now about the status of someone's character development.

***

Change is possible but it is neither easy nor a straightforward process.

***

The Work of Change

Any change in behavior takes work, and disturbed characters often have dysfunctional and socially problematic attitudes toward work. For most of us, work is not only a perceived necessity but also, many times, a life's passion and a means to personal fulfillment. And for those of us fortunate enough to be involved in an enterprise that makes the best use of our talents and allows us to make a meaningful social contribution to boot, our work can be a most rewarding experience. But unfortunately, for some individuals work is truly a dirty little word.

There are several personality types notorious not only for their distaste for work, but also for the negative impact that their distaste for work has on society. And two of the most problematic aggressive personality types—the unbridled aggressive (i.e., antisocial) personality and the predatory aggressive (i.e., psychopathic or sociopathic) personality—are in part defined by their seriously dysfunctional attitudes toward work.

It's not that the problem personalities among us won't work at all. True, some are, for lack of better words, lazy and parasitic (e.g., some antisocial and sociopathic types), but even these folks can sometimes put out considerable sweat and effort. What they really resist is engaging in the kind of work that for most of us is begotten out of a sense of social obligation. They simply detest putting out effort that might, even in part, benefit someone else. They're quite capable of spending inordinate amounts time and energy working purely to get something they want. A criminal type of personality, for example, might spend weeks casing a particular place of business, taking careful notes, and concocting elaborate plans to rob it successfully. But putting the same amount of energy into finding or keeping a legitimate job, demonstrating the loyalty and consistency necessary to be considered for advancement, or making the investment in personal self-development to merit consideration for more advanced position are completely different matters, and most unattractive enterprises.

Problematic attitudes toward work are hallmarks of many disturbed characters, not just some of the aggressive personalities. Some problem characters (e.g., those with narcissistic traits) feel too entitled to anything they want to feel a sufficient sense of obligation to really earn things. Others (e.g., manipulative con artists) derive far more satisfaction from the idea of getting something for nothing or by swindling someone else than they can possibly get from putting in an honest day's work. Still others have outright contempt for work, especially if the work's primary purpose is something other than pure self-benefit (e.g., caring for one's family, contributing to society, etc.).

Perhaps the toughest job any of us has in life is the work it takes to develop our own character. None of us is born perfect. We all have our strengths and weaknesses, some of which are naturally endowed. And we all have our share of hardships to overcome. So the greatest single challenge we face is reckoning with ourselves in such a way that we make of ourselves a productive, contributing, and respect-worthy person. Disturbed characters resist this kind of work more than any other. Why? Because even contemplating such an undertaking is too much like putting someone or something else ahead of purely selfish desires. And for the character-impaired individual, nothing is as important to them as what they want. Besides, wanting something for nothing is another hallmark. So even when it comes to respect, they want to come by that in the same manner as everything else: without having to earn it.

Making the choice in one's heart to be the best one can be for the welfare of all requires an uncommon level of dedication and commitment. And there's absolutely no reason to submit to this arduous and life-long undertaking unless one has a deep and underlying sense of social obligation. But doing the work of character development can be another one of those labors of love. It certainly takes a lot of love to do it. It's ironic that l-o-v-e is also a four-letter word. But it just doesn't have the same connotation to people of integrity that w-o-r-k does for the impaired characters among us.

The Work of Change: Why Insight Is Never Enough

Insight is great, but without challenging and confronting dysfunctional thinking and behavior patterns, and most especially, without reinforcing efforts to do things differently, most people will stay feeling "stuck." With most disturbed characters, however, insight or the lack thereof is not the issue. They see but disagree. It is necessary for them to change their mind and start thinking and, consequently, believing, and acting differently. But even in the case where someone has only a mild character disturbance and some neurosis, or perhaps even the case where someone is mostly neurotic and therefore the need and potential benefit from insight is higher, insight alone is never enough for change to occur.

It never ceases to amaze me how much insight a person can gain within the therapeutic milieu. It is always rewarding to witness someone finally "put all the pieces together" as to how they got the way they were. But my psychotherapy clients have taught me (a lesson also validated by ample research) that most of the time, insight simply isn't enough when it comes to changing one's life. In fact, the fact that someone might have come to "see" the self-defeating things they do as well as why (based on the emotional scars of the past) they do them, yet continue to have difficulty doing things differently can, in itself, be a significant source of distress. A person can easily wonder if they wouldn't have been better off remaining in the dark. As one client so aptly put the dilemma: "I know what I do and why I do it, and I know what I need to do instead, so why can't I seem to make myself do it? It makes me crazy!" To address that concern, I often find myself drawing upon lessons I've learned from my work with disturbed characters. Insight is great but without challenging dysfunctional thinking and behavior patterns, and most especially, without reinforcing efforts to do things differently, most people will stay "stuck," feeling better only for the few moments that they have the opportunity to "vent" their frustration during the therapy hour.

***

**Insight isn't enough when it comes to changing
one's life and relationships.**

***

Covert self-monitoring and self-reinforcement are powerful instruments in the process of change. Such tools make the work of changing one's usual *modus operandi* easier and help the client develop increased motivation to persist in the effort to change. But there can be a high cost of change that can "hang" people up in their quest to do better, and there is value of doing a change cost/benefit analysis of a person's behavior patterns and implementing strategies that lower the cost of change.

Adherents of traditional approaches stress the importance of "working through" the "dynamics" (Jung used the term "complexes") during talk therapy even after the client gains awareness. But even this process is more of an internal emotional reconciliation of sorts and not an automatic change in one's behavior. The fact is, once we develop certain ways of doing things — whatever the reasons were for us developing them in the first place — it's really hard to change course. Old habits are simply really hard to break, and as we know from learning theory, nothing is ever really "unlearned." Even when we learn new behaviors and begin to implement them, it's always likely that we'll fall back into old patterns from time to time. That's why it's so important not only to reinforce ourselves as we strive to do better but to confer that reinforcement on our sincere effort.

Some behavioral therapists have long argued that insight is unnecessary for change. Others have argued it has little real value, while still others, especially those working within the cognitive-behavioral framework, argue that once a person comes to some awareness about why they've made the choices they have, they're freer to make new, better choices. Some have suggested that while insight is indeed important to self-understanding, it need not be pursued as a primary objective in therapy.

Increased awareness, it's been argued, can and often does come on the heels of doing things differently. It's a kind of "taste and see" approach to learning. Do the thing you fear to do or are not naturally inclined to do, and you'll see what a difference it can make. My experience has shown me that while this is true, the insight that can be gained from doing things differently can extend well beyond just becoming aware of a new reality. In pushing oneself to do differently, one always has to confront the demons of the past that fuel the resistance to change. Often, in confronting that resistance head-on, a person can come into full conscious contact with issues they have long repressed. When this happens, I encourage my clients to find yet another reason to reinforce themselves, because not only has their effort to do better paid off behaviorally, it's afforded them a level of awareness and understanding they didn't have before, and the fruits of both these things are only likely to increase over time.

Insight by itself rarely makes change possible. But with commitment and hard work (and a lot of reinforcement), a person can not only change and grow but also acquire a greater level of self-awareness. Perhaps it's true that insight does not equal cure. But in my experience, they go together.

Take Away

Change is possible but it is neither easy nor a straightforward process. It takes work. And sometimes the amount of change a person can undergo is severely limited, but patience, tenacity, and reinforcement are required. How do you know someone is honestly trying to change? There is a difference in the person's behavior and their willingness to altruistically put someone else's needs and wants ahead of their own. Insight into why a person does what he does, is important, but is not sufficient nor does it substitute for the work of change.

Empowerment Tools

1. As people mature with time and experience, they change; even though there is a continuity in who they are at their core.

2. With sound cognitive-behavioral intervention and the help of appropriate medication when necessary, even some of the most dysfunctional personalities can be modified.

3. No one has to stay "stuck" in their old habits. But when we learn new behaviors and begin to implement them, it's always likely that we'll fall back into old patterns from time to time. That's why it's so important not only to reinforce ourselves as we strive to do better but to also reward our sincere effort.

4. Patience and trust go a long way to help people change. But healthy confrontation is an indispensable tool to keep everyone honest and on the right road.

5. The best way to know if someone has changed is how that person behaves in the here and now.

Chapter Eight
Do I Stay or Should I Go?

As you take an honest look at how your relationship has gotten to where it is today, you might realize that making the right assessment of a person's character before getting involved in a serious relationship is more important than ever, because there are so many disturbed people. Each type of character exhibits certain, reliable signs (in patterns of interpersonal behavior, dominant attitudes, and ways of thinking about things), and if you know what to look for, you can possibly stave off disaster.

Amy and Jack

The story Amy and Jack is instructive, and it illustrates the kind of trouble that can ensue when you don't take a good look at the character of the person you're involved with.

I first became acquainted with Amy after a friend suggested she seek me out. She called and set an appointment for her and her husband Jack. Amy and Jack had seen a therapist a little over a year ago and Amy was disappointed in the results. She tried to understand when the therapist said that Jack must have grown up lacking the approval he needed, especially from his mother and the other significant women in his life, that he had a deep fear of genuine intimacy and commitment, and that his cheating was a way to get the affirmation he craved and to build his self-esteem. And she worked really hard doing her part to allay those fears, but things were still not working out. She thought she could get past the fact he had two affairs; but now, even after therapy, and even after all her hard work, everything was going wrong again. The lies, the constant wondering, the rants, and the denials that made her feel like she was crazy—they were all back. She just couldn't understand or take much more of what she feared would be his constant unfaithfulness. All sense of trust was gone. She also felt both used and discarded. She wanted more out of life and a relationship but somehow felt guilty and selfish about it. From time to time she did think she might have to leave because of how hard it was to bear the hurt. But she'd invested so much of herself trying to make things work, and there were occasional glimmers of hope, so she couldn't bring herself to simply walk away.

When we met, Amy's and Jack's demeanor told me a lot before we even began talking. Amy appeared anxious for help, while Jack appeared not only disinterested but a bit put off by the whole thing. Still, Jack did a lot of the talking, right from the outset. He wanted to know what good it might do to come to sessions, how much I charged, and he made it clear that he believed that the reason they were in my office was because Amy was "never satisfied" and expected "far too much" in their relationship. He was a "damned good provider" and she had all the money and comforts a person could possibly want, so he couldn't understand what all the big fuss was about. He said that he told Amy about the two affairs even before they saw their first counselor, but he went on to say that he was "stressed" at work at the time and wasn't feeling appreciated at home. He also insisted that his dalliances "meant nothing at all" and that Amy's "paranoia" was not only unwarranted but had recently gotten "out of bounds."

I asked Jack what he had done to repair the damage he'd done by breaching the trust in his relationship with Amy. His immediate reply was "Huh?" That told me a lot, all by itself. But to add insult to injury, he quickly added: "Well, she was supposed to quit snooping and questioning me all the time. And she was also supposed to give me some positive attention—that's what the therapist said she should do. But did she do it? No! She's still sneaking around trying to check my cell phone and emails all the time. I even had to close one email account and open another just to have some privacy!" Jack seemed outraged and indignant. But he didn't seem like someone who felt horrible about having injured the love of his life. There was no remorse for his actions nor was there any willingness to make amends. It was all on Amy. These were immediate and clearly present signs of character disturbance and my observations correlated with his behavioral history.

By the end of the interview I'd managed to learn at least five things.

1. Jack actually came from a loving, caring family who pretty much gave him everything, including more attention and approval than anyone might ever need.

2. He had always been a thrill-seeker, being quite the daredevil most of his young life and was just as heavily into fast cars as he was into "fast" and "willing" women.

3. He had crossed many other lines and boundaries than merely those pertaining to his marital vows. In fact, he'd engaged in enough shady practices in his business that, were it not for his wealth, means, shrewdness, and access to top-notch lawyers, he might well be in jail.

4. He had many more "dalliances" than the two he confessed during his prior therapy stint, and since that time he had had numerous others. He got "careless" with his texting on his cell phone which is how Amy's suspicions recently became aroused again.

5. He saw absolutely nothing wrong with his behavior. The women meant nothing to him, and, from his point of view, he had given Amy "everything a woman could possibly want." He had "absolutely nothing to feel guilty about."

This was a man of such deficient character that he couldn't possibly conduct a relationship on the plane to which Amy aspired. And he'd been this way since adolescence. Moreover, after listening to Amy describe why and how she fell in love with him, it was clear she had virtually no ability to accurately appraise his character or anyone else's for that matter. Of course, the stint in therapy didn't help matters on that count either, for this was not a self-esteem deficient, approval-hungry, wounded soul who deeply feared commitment because his mother never loved him enough (as the therapist suggested), but rather a self-indulgent, empathy-devoid, remorseless thrill-seeker, people exploiter and abuser, and serial boundary and rule violator. A man without remorse and devoid of real contrition. So trusting the therapist's judgment on things only made matters worse. Only lately was Amy becoming more willing to listen to her own inner voice, which had long been trying to tell her what kind of person she was really dealing with. But she was too afraid and unsure of herself to act on what she was slowly coming to realize.

I worked with Amy a relatively short time, considering how much she needed to change with respect to the way she viewed herself, her worth, and how she judged the character of others. But once, as they say, the light bulb moment happened—her *Aha!*—she was on a roll. She dealt with her own character issues, especially her emotional dependency and feelings of inadequacy, then found her strength and got her bearings. Then she made a commitment to never sell herself so short again or give herself away so cheaply. It's a commitment she's kept to this day.

Emma and Paul

Emma was probably one of the most beautiful women Paul had ever laid eyes on. And she was ever so charming and outgoing. Everybody liked her, although no one seemed to know her all that well. Paul was so excited the first time she agreed to meet him over coffee that he could hardly contain himself. And it wasn't long that they began dating steadily, and not long afterward that Emma indicated she wouldn't mind moving in with Paul.

Paul didn't know a whole lot about Emma, but he felt he knew enough. She was bright, charming, and so much fun to be with. She had two young children, who would also be moving in, but she seemed really good with them and they seemed like great kids. Besides, he liked the children and they seemed to like him too. He didn't know all that much about Emma's prior relationships, except that she married "way too young," and had lived with two other men who turned out to be "creeps." She also had run up lots of debt. But she had good explanations for that too. Her last boyfriend was laid off from his job twice and never did his fair share while they were together. Emma was bearing her burdens all alone, and her paycheck simply couldn't cover all the bills and the kids' needs.

Paul fell for Emma and her story of bad luck. She was estranged from her parents who threw her out when she was eighteen. She just never seemed to catch a break. Paul didn't mind paying off her credit cards and helping her out. He felt sorry for her, and he had to admit, it felt really good to feel so appreciated. Emma was good about showing her affection, too. She made him feel both valued and needed.

Then after a few weeks it happened; Emma didn't come home until the next morning. Paul was pretty much in a state of shock for days. He had been frantic with worry about what could have happened to her. And it was insult on top of injury when it became clear how "high" she was when she eventually did show up. How could she do this to him, he wondered? And how could she just leave the kids? Just who was this woman, who just days ago he thought was so wonderful?

Eventually Paul would learn that Emma's story about being "thrown out" and abandoned by her "emotionally abusive" parents at age eighteen wasn't accurate. In reality, her parents, were decent folks who tried to get her help in adolescence but she was always non-compliant. They even had her admitted to an inpatient facility that had an intensive program. But when she turned eighteen, they could no longer force the issue of treatment. They told her she could live with them if she observed reasonable rules and limits, but Emma had a mind of her own. Emma's parents didn't abandon her. Rather she bolted when faced with the prospect of having to submit herself to rules and authority.

Paul also learned that the pills Emma always had around for her "fibromyalgia" weren't really legitimately prescribed medicines and that she had a history of abusing multiple substances. And he eventually learned that the reason she didn't come home was because she'd spent the night with an old boyfriend. He also found out that her two children were not from her first marriage as he was led to believe, but rather the result of indiscretions during the times she lived with her prior two boyfriends. And by the time he realized he needed to end the relationship immediately and take back the duplicate bankcard he'd given her for household expenses, his account had been cleaned out.

Eventually, Paul would learn a lot about himself, especially the things that make him vulnerable to exploitation and prone to making inadequate judgments about a person's character. Paul always wants to see the best in people, but he also tends to be too trusting and to take things at face value. And when his gut is churning—like all those times when he would ask Emma about things and her answers were so vague that he never really felt like he got a real answer—he doesn't give enough credence to his feeling that something's amiss. He's also the kind of guy who's so genuinely insecure that when an attractive woman shows him attention and interest, any good judgment he might otherwise have goes straight out the window. He's a "soft touch" whose poor judgment allowed him to be taken to the cleaners. But warning signs were always there if he'd simply been a bit more objective: a failed marriage, at least two other failed relationships, estranged family, and financial irresponsibility. (The history of irresponsible sexual behavior could have been easily flushed out as well with just a little probing.) And while it's possible that all these things could have had a perfectly legitimate explanation, the fact that they were present begged for Paul's more ardent investigation. If he'd done his homework and really gotten to know the character of the person he was hooking up with, he'd have spared himself a lot of heartache and saved a lot of money.

Paul learned that manipulation tactics Emma used: the careful use of vagueness as a means of deceit, adept display of superficial charm and other forms of seduction, always having excuses or rationalizations for problem behaviors, and ready externalization of blame. But if he had been more savvy, he might have spotted certain thinking errors, such as circumstantial thinking and hard-luck thinking. These things would have been a tip-off that he was dealing with someone of disturbed character. Paul knows these things now, but he didn't know them in time to avoid being taken in by Emma. He also understands that in order to judge the character of others objectively and accurately, you also have to know yourself pretty well.

Interestingly, even though Emma was in treatment on several occasions, her diagnoses spanned the gamut from depression, post-traumatic stress disorder, histrionic personality traits, but her diagnosis never included either conduct disorder or personality or character disorder. If Emma were male, it's quite likely someone would have entertained the possibility she had a narcissistic or antisocial personality disorder. It seems that when it comes to making sound judgments about character-impaired females, professionals sometimes have as much trouble as do potential relationship partners. And one of the purposes of this book has been to help you ask the right questions, gather the right information, and look for the telltale signs that someone's character poses big problems for any relationship you're considering having with them.

But as you read this book, it may all come down to this one question: Do I stay or should I go? It may be too late to be forewarned, and you might be asking yourself if confronting your loved one is worth it. Should I just leave things alone? Maybe he/she won't change and I should just learn to live with it? Maybe I should just chalk it up to experience and move on? These are all legitimate questions and only you can decide. This book offers you tools, but you are the one to decide how to or if you want to use them.

Or maybe you are the disturbed person yourself. Might your loved ones be better off if you just left? Or might it be less painful for everybody if you left?

Well-informed decisions are always preferable to ill-advised plans, but consider this: you may leave this relationship but unless you change, chances are that you'll end up with someone else just like the person you left. There are good reasons we end up with the people we do, but that is the subject of another book. For now, let's consider a couple of common questions people ask when they are trying to make a final decision.

If I Let Him Know I Know Why He's Doing Things to Hurt Me, Will He Stop?

This question comes from Vicky, a reader of my blog. (Details and names have been altered to protect anonymity.)

> I'm not a psychologist or medical person, but when my boyfriend flipped out on me for no apparent reason, I knew something was wrong. I think he has a phobia. My boyfriend always wears sunglasses and has about ten pairs of them. He won't even go into certain establishments if wearing sunglasses is prohibited. I believe he does this to avoid eye contact with people. He also avoids certain social situations. Being with a crowd of people he doesn't know makes him very uncomfortable. I love him and he has asked me many times, while under the influence, to marry him. Yet, when I remind him, he gets angry. He yells at me and says things to insult me and hurt my feelings. Yet he can also be so sweet, caring and playful. It's really confusing. Every time we start to get close, he pushes me away. It's like he sabotages our relationship. I believe what he does and not what he says, so I don't let the things that he says bother me so much. However, I also believe that I am letting him take control of my life. I thought about it and have decided to confront him with what I believe his problem is. I feel if I tell him that I know what he's doing by being mean to me, maybe I can take the control away, and he'll stop because he'll know that it's not affecting me. But then again I fear that it might make him go deeper into his shell and never speak to me again. Do you think that I should tell him?

This is a common question: If I tell him why do does mean things, will he stop? We need to be really cautious about making interpretations about the "underlying reasons" for inappropriate behavior. It's possible that Vicky is right about her boyfriend's "phobia" of commitment that causes him to "sabotage" things when they start to "get close." Such presumptions and interpretations have often been among the reasons people allow themselves to enter or stay in abusive relationships. Instead of kidding herself and maintaining the "illusion" of control by thinking she has the power to know and expose her partner's motives and therefore take away his "reasons" for his dysfunctional behavior, Vicky needs to take actual control of her own life by setting limits, expectations, enforcing boundaries, and most especially by paying attention to people's behavior as the best predictor of what they will do in the future. Maybe she should just let go.

***

It's never simple or easy to just forgive and forget.

***

Should I Change My Whole Life for Someone Who Doesn't Seem to Give Anything?

Here is another frequently asked question: Should I change my whole life for someone who doesn't seem to care about me? This question is from Yolanda. (Name and details altered.)

> I am in a long-distance relationship. He wants me to quit my job and move to where he lives—hundreds of miles away. This means leaving my family and friends, moving my sons away from their father, and so on. We communicate mostly online. I can see from his Facebook page that he talks to other women quite often. I've told him that I'm uncomfortable with this, but he says I'm just trying to control him. He doesn't seem willing to give up anything for me but wants me to change my whole life for him. Lately, he does not even tell me what he is doing and says it's because I will only "get mad" if I know. This makes me feel anxious. I don't like the way he treats me. Why would he be keeping things from me? I don't feel like we're really communicating. He doesn't seem to care about my feelings, and he doesn't want to talk about what he is doing. I also don't get any sense

that he wants to be fair. What should I do?
Because I don't want to control him, but I
certainly do want my feelings acknowledged
and to be cared about as much as he wants me
to care for him.

Any relationship has pros and cons; let's look at some of them. On the con side, there's the emotional hardship of leaving family and friends, moving to a strange location, putting greater distance between Yolanda's sons and their father, being with a man she doesn't really know that well or fully trust and is anxious about, entering a relationship where she gives everything and he concedes nothing, experiencing a lack of communication, and not having her feelings acknowledged or respected.

Then on the pro side, there's...uh...uh...oh, wait! I don't see any! Yolanda needs to let go.

Seven Secrets of Letting Go

There are millions of reasons why people hang onto relationships. And as challenging as it can be to move on from a bad emotional experience, it's not uncommon for folks who have undergone trying circumstances or experienced trauma of some kind to have difficulty letting go emotionally and moving on with life. Such difficulties are especially common in the aftermath of a toxic relationship. Letting go of a relationship, which has been painful but in which you've nonetheless been heavily invested, is never an easy task. Sometimes that's because the emotional wounds are still fresh, and you're not of a mind to forgive the person or persons you believe inflicted those wounds. Sometimes, it's because you're not ready to forgive yourself. You might wonder how you could have been so naïve or foolish to have allowed yourself to get into or remain in your situation. You might be beating yourself up emotionally for not knowing better. Still other times, your difficulty letting go has more to do with the natural tendency to remain with what you're familiar, so that you don't have the even more daunting task of facing the unknown.

All this emotional and behavioral paralysis comes with a price: continued victimization. Still, as anyone who's been in a bad situation knows, it's neither simple nor easy to embrace the well-known adage to "forgive and forget." Make no mistake, moving on almost always involves much more than merely forgiving and forgetting. It requires properly attending to your wounds, finding the proper avenues for healing, and then embarking on the tough task of claiming and forging a new and more empowered life. All this takes energy, which in many cases has already been significantly depleted.

As challenging as it can be to move on from a bad emotional experience, there are some fairly straightforward things anyone can do to make the process a bit easier. Over the years, many folks have shared with me their secrets for getting "unstuck" and moving forward. Here are seven.

1. Take an Objective Step Back

Spending months or years immersed in the trials of a problematic relationship can cause you to lose all sense of objectivity. You can even lose sight of what "normal" is. You have to distance yourself from the conflict you've been in to see the reality of it more realistically. So it's important to take time out from thinking or stewing about the mess you've been in and to do your best to look at things from a distance. Before long, you'll begin to see that mess and the world around you in a much different light.

2. Reframe

Take some different perspectives on the ordeal you've been through. Most especially, reframe as many of the more negative aspects of your experience as you can into perceptions of a positive character. For example, change the thought that you've been played for a fool to the thought that you've been given the opportunity for new insights and a renewed appreciation of what really matters to you. Putting a positive slant on negative perceptions is not easy, and you might even find yourself not believing in what you're doing at first. But sometimes you have to "fake it to make it." With time, changing the way you see things from negative to positive will provide you with some increased motivation and energy to move on.

3. *Accept the Lessons of the Past and Learn and Profit from Them*

Life is all about learning and growing. As hard as it can be to accept at times, there are always valuable lessons to be learned from even the most unpleasant of experiences. But before you can truly profit from a situation you have to accept and embrace all that the experience has to inform and teach you. Sometimes, that's a really difficult thing to, do but the potential payoffs are substantial.

4. *Redirect Your Focus*

Dealing with difficult circumstances can get you into the habit of focusing your attention and energy externally. For some people, this is the very "formula" for depression, which can further hinder you from moving forward in your life. To really empower yourself to move on, you need to get in greater touch with your wants, needs, desires, aspirations, etc. So when you find yourself focusing externally, especially on people, places, and things you can't control, it's important to redirect your attention inward. And because you always have the power to do something differently, it's best to focus your attention and energy on taking action. The type or size of the steps you take to make things different is nowhere near as important as merely taking some kind of action. Over time, step-by-step, and before you know it, you'll be breaking the chains of emotional bondage and moving forward.

5. *Uncover Then Face Your Fears*

Many times, we remain ensconced with the familiar old junk in our lives because we're actually afraid of moving forward. Much of the time, just what we fear is not fully conscious. The unknown is always scary, so taking the time to reflect on what we might be afraid of and facing that fear head on can mean the difference between remaining stuck and claiming a new life.

6. *Make Peace with—and Cut—Your Losses*

Before we get to the point where we know we have to exit a bad situation, we've often invested a lot of time and energy trying to make things work. It's really hard to walk away from such an investment. I call this phenomenon the "slot machine syndrome." To move forward you must first make peace with the fact that your prior decisions have come with a price (in time, energy, and often, money) and then resolve to cut your losses. This can make the difference between feeling completely "taken" and learning a costly but nonetheless invaluable lesson.

7. *Seize and Value the Moment*

You cannot re-live yesterday and you really have no power over tomorrow. It's important to stay in the here and now. There's no greater power than the power of now. Just recognizing and accepting that fact is empowering in itself. Once you experience the value of seizing every moment, it becomes much easier to keep your eyes forward and to resist the temptation to look back.

Letting go and moving on is a tough task for sure. But it's a task made so much easier when you know the secrets to getting unstuck and moving forward. Hopefully, these tips from those who've been there will prove helpful to anyone who has been through some tough times and is having some difficulty letting go.

Toxic Relationship Aftermath

Even when a person lets go, there are still consequences and perhaps wounds from the relationship, especially if the relationship is toxic. It is clear in questions asked at the beginning of this chapter that both women found themselves in a relationship with a disturbed person. They might well ask themselves, why? People get into relationships with disturbed characters for a variety of reasons. They might be somewhat naïve about human nature, having an essentially Pollyanna-like vision of others, and never fully appreciating the extent to which some people's character can be so flawed that a relationship with them is destined to be toxic. They might also have been over-exposed to and blindly accepted some of our older, traditional psychological perspectives that tend to view everyone as basically good and decent "underneath"; and, therefore, judged the hurtful behaviors of their relationship partner as merely the unfortunate manifestation of that person's emotional wounding and trauma. So, even if they noticed some red-flags for trouble early on, they might have entertained the notion that with enough patience, love, and understanding, the partner's wounds would necessarily be healed and all would be well. Love, after all, conquers all—does it not? But many relational abuse survivors have simply been the unwitting victims of a masterful con artist who said all the right things and did all the right things on the front end of the relationship to secure the object of his/her desire, only to reveal their true self once their conquest was complete and they found little reason to perpetuate their fraud any longer.

***

**Even if a person lets go, bad relationships
can still leave emotional scars.**

***

Once folks get into a relationship with a disturbed character, it's often not so easy to get out, even when things get really bad at times. For one thing, disturbed characters are often not only determined to win or dominate but also have the skills to manipulate others and keep them in one-down positions and under their control. And perhaps even more insidiously, the aggrieved party in a dysfunctional relationship often invests considerable time and energy (and sometimes considerable financial and other personal resources) trying to make things work. Infrequent but nonetheless significant and periodic "rewards" for making such an investment make it even more likely the abused party will stay involved. So even when the situation has become too toxic and painful to bear anymore, breaking free means walking away from a substantial personal investment, and reckoning with such a loss is not an easy thing to do. And reckoning with the need to get out also invites understandable (albeit unwarranted) feelings of guilt and shame for having allowed oneself to be duped in the first place.

Most people I've counseled, who've finally reached the point that they simply had to extricate themselves from a toxic relationship, appeared as though they'd been run over by a train. And in those cases where the disturbed character vowed all sorts of nastiness if divorce was pursued as the ultimate solution, the victim had virtually no energy left to weather the brutal battle they knew lay ahead. They were deeply depressed and desperate for support. And it was not particularly sweet music to their ears to hear me advise that they do their best to "let go" of the inordinate attention they'd focused on their abuser. After all, they had finally come to identify the true source of their pain and wanted to hold their tormentor accountable. So, the notion of emotionally letting go of the other person and taking stock in themselves was not initially appealing at all. But in time, and with sufficient support and encouragement, they saw more clearly that they were their own key to a richer, empowered life.

These cons are clever, calculated, and smooth. They are hard to rattle. At the end of one of these nightmares even the person who went in to the situation relatively healthy and intact comes out drained, shaken, weakened, confused, and often too exhausted to fight for their honor. It's hard to remember all the twists and turns, let alone describe them in context. SO MUCH gets lost in translation.

One person told me that his "sociopathic ex was just skipping right along and never missed a beat. Meanwhile I was feeling like I got hit head-on by a Mac truck. My life was turned upside down because so much of my time was eaten up with her."

Lynn (not her real name) was an upper-middle class wife and mother of four sons. Her life, she said, wasn't perfect but it was good enough. She initially came to see me because she suspected her husband was having an affair at work. She knew something was wrong but couldn't put her finger on it. The next time she had an appointment, she, not only, knew that her husband was having an affair, but he had emptied their bank account, and she had no money to buy groceries (or her session). As time went by, he moved in and out of the house trying to decide his course of action. Then he hit on an idea, Lynn was the problem so she could just find another place to live. He would stay put with the boys and get on with his life. Lynn found herself with no money, no job skills, and no visitation rights to see her children. When I saw her again months later, she had managed to find a low-paying waitressing job, but, at least she wasn't starving, and she could occasionally see the boys with supervision. Needless to say, Lynn was beat up emotionally and physically worn out from working ten-hour shifts. She told me that not only had her ex-husband remarried, but that he remarried someone who looked a lot like her but younger. Lynn had been betrayed, humiliated, discarded, and abandoned. She would have liked to confront her ex-husband, but she was too exhausted.

If only we could learn to trust those early "pings" of unease and warning that our intuition sends! Disturbed characters know how to care about people's well-being, but they just care more about their own well-being than that of others. It's really about the misuse of power, not about immaturity or lack of skills. They experience payoffs by bullying other people, and these rewards are so valued by them that they rarely find the motivation to change.

***

Letting go of a relationship is never easy, but it is doable.

***

Torn Apart, Scarred, but Moving On

The decision whether to stay or leave a relationship can be difficult under any circumstance, but when sexual intimacy is involved, complications multiply. Psychologists have long known that sexual intimacy is a form of emotional bonding not just physical. When two people are intimate, there is a lasting physiological bonding that takes place. It is true that physical intimacy means different things to men and women, and it is also true that sexual intimacy is more than physical closeness. But there is also true that in the sexual act, two people in a real sense become one. And when those persons break up, their oneness is torn apart, leaving an emotional wound that will eventually scar, making the next sexual encounter with another person more difficult. It can get to the place where a person has bonded, torn apart, wounded, and scarred so often that true intimacy with anyone becomes impossible. That is a tragedy of prostitution and promiscuity.

Bill wanted to settle down and get married. He was thirty-four and had "been around." But Bill was worried, which is why he came to see me. Bill had had so many sexual encounters, one-night-stands, and dating relationships, that meaningful, fulfilling sex didn't exist for him. But he was tired and bored with his lifestyle. He had broken up with so many women that he'd lost track. But now, he said, he was ready to take on adult responsibilities, except first he believed that he needed a wife. His presenting problem was what kind of girl should he look for? He thought if he found a virgin everything would be ok. It took many sessions for Bill to sort things out and actually feel remorse for how he'd hurt a lot of women. Needless to say marrying a virgin wasn't the answer, because how he had lived had diminished his capacity for intimacy with anyone.

People feel bonded to their sexual partner, because they are. And when partners break up, there is grief and the need for healing, no matter how great the sex was. This is an oversimplification, but sexual intimacy is like glue that keeps people together. Severing this tie between two people can never be clean. There is no such thing as a clean break for most people. All break-ups are messy.

Whether you stay or go, there will be wounds that need tending. Give yourself the time to heal before you launch into another relationship.

Take Away

As challenging as it can be to move on from a bad relationship, it's not uncommon to have difficulty letting go emotionally and moving on with life. Such difficulties are especially common in the aftermath of a toxic relationship. Letting go of a relationship, which has been painful but in which you've nonetheless been heavily invested, is never an easy task. But it is doable.

Empowerment Tools

The seven secrets to letting go:

1. Take an objective step back.

2. Reframe.

3. Accept the lessons of the past and learn and profit from them.

4. Redirect your focus.

5. Uncover then face your fears.

6. Make peace with — and cut — your losses.

7. Seize and value the moment.

Chapter Nine
Change Your Game

Perhaps you ask yourself: "Why do I always seem to end up in a relationship with a disturbed character? I've just gotten out of one bad relationship, how can I avoid getting into another?" To thrive in a character-disturbed world, perhaps you need to become a better judge of character and know the terms of engagement of the kind of people you're dealing with. This chapter will give you some game changers that can go a long way to empowering you to do what you need to do, whether it is to work on your relationship or let go and try again.

By changing your game, I don't mean that you need to have better gamesmanship or that relationships are something we play with. I don't mean to minimize the importance of relationships, but I do mean that you can change the way you behave, make more informed decisions, plan more effectively, and act more assertively. You can change the terms of engagement, the way you interact in order to have healthier relationships in the future.

Becoming a Better Judge of Character

Establishing and maintaining healthy, productive relationships is fundamental to human existence and happiness. And the impact certain kinds of relationships can have upon us simply cannot be understated. Loving, supportive, and nurturing relationships have a certain character to them. And of course, the character of the individuals in a relationship has a lot to do with what the overall tone that any particular relationship has. That's why it's important to take your time and become a good or better judge of character.

Many survivors of an abusive or otherwise toxic relationship live in fear of making a fatal mistake again. They also question how they got themselves into their bad situation in the first place. They become unsure of their judgment, and this can leave them feeling confused, lost, mistrusting, and even paranoid. Adequately judging character is no easy business. It's not even easy for professionals with years of training and experience, which is just one reason why some professionals choose to ignore the issue. But in our times of widespread character disturbance, being a good judge of character is more important than ever. You simply must know what kind of person you're dealing with and how to spot the red flags that getting involved with them will invite trouble.

It wasn't too long ago that most folks in the Western world still observed some traditions cultivated over centuries to help individuals "vet" candidates for serious relationships. Dating, courtship, and formal engagement were commonly part of this process. Dating was often conducted both in the company of and under the supervision of trusted friends and sometimes even official chaperones. This was to keep the purpose of dating focused on becoming acquainted as opposed to all the other possibilities. After a period of dating, formal courtship might ensue. If things got "serious," a marriage proposal might be expected and the couple, with the family's blessing (i.e., the family believed that at least the minimum requirements were met for a person to be a potential marriage partner) would become engaged. And during the period of official engagement, not only would the couple get to know each other more intimately (as the result of more frequent contact), but the extended family would have an even greater opportunity to scrutinize the potential marriage partner for behavior patterns, attitudes, and other proclivities that might signal trouble ahead. Even then, built into most marriage ceremonies was the fabled anxiety-raising question about whether anyone attending the ceremony knew of any reason whatsoever why it might not be a good idea for the couple to seal their vows, followed by an exhortation to speak up quickly so that potential disaster could be avoided. Marriage was taken very seriously and wasn't entered into lightly.

We may views these traditions as idealized, antiquated, unnecessary, and even perhaps harmful. After all we are not Victorian, living in the nineteenth or even twentieth centuries. Relationships these days are very different. All the definitions of what we once thought we knew are changing. And while a case can be made about the benefits flowing from the increased freedom folks have in selecting and entering into relationships, it would certainly be fair to say that these days we have the extreme opposite: relationships are entered into far too casually and for less than optimal reasons, which is why they so often fall apart so quickly or turn out to be so dysfunctional.

I've counseled hundreds of couples over the years. And I've always asked each spouse to give the top three reasons they had for getting involved with their partner. I can tell you the answers, though sometimes hard to comprehend, no longer shock me but are always very telling. Still, even when a person is fairly conscientious about entering into a relationship, it's possible to be fooled or blindsided. That's because some disturbed characters are so adept at the art of impression management. They know how to pull the wool over your eyes and win you over. In short, they know how to get what they want; but once they have it, there's less need for pretenses, and that's when all the trouble usually begins.

The surest way to avoid potential victimization is to know the basic personality types and exactly what makes each type of character tick. So if you decide to confront someone, you must prepare yourself by knowing the kind of person you are dealing with, how to assess their character, and how your concern for others can be used against you, especially if your partner is disturbed.

Avoid Letting Others Take Advantage of You

When someone engages in a behavior that's a problem, the reason they do it is irrelevant. If we try too hard to understand the behavior, before long we'll find ourselves excusing it and eventually enabling it. This chapter will discuss the keys to empowering oneself not only in relationships with disturbed characters, but in all social interactions. There are two major keys to personal empowerment.

1. Recognize the pitfalls of traditionally-accepted explanations for why people do the things they do.

2. Adopt a new framework for understanding the underpinnings of behavior—especially the behavior of individuals of deficient or disturbed character.

Once these main principles are grasped, there are specific methods or tools a person can employ to keep from being taken advantage of in relationships with unscrupulous characters. This chapter will take a look at each of these tools and how to apply them in everyday situations. These empowerment tools might also be called "terms of engagement" with those who might otherwise attempt to manipulate or take advantage of you.

***

**When people engage in problematic behavior,
the reason they do it is irrelevant.**

***

One of the most problematic legacies of traditional psychology is the notion that people's behavior is largely motivated by their fears and insecurities and that they are not often consciously aware of their emotional "issues." Most of us are familiar with the tenets of traditional psychology. So when somebody does something unnerving, we almost always try to understand it by asking ourselves what need, fear, or insecurity underlies it. Worst of all, often the leap is made from "understanding" the behavior to inadvertently excusing it or "enabling" it.

Game Changer: Accept No Excuses

The single most important game changer is to "accept no excuses" for hurtful, harmful, or inappropriate behavior. Once a person stops trying to explain or understand a behavior and simply sets a limit to no longer accept it, everything begins to change. Learning to correctly identify and label the various problem behaviors that disturbed characters frequently display as well as learning how to respond to those behaviors is equally empowering.

As I mentioned above, when someone engages in a behavior that's a problem, the reason they do it is irrelevant. If a behavior is wrong, it needs to be corrected, pure and simple. And we need to hold one another accountable. It's the only way to stem the stunningly rising tide of character disturbance in our culture. We complete the process of empowerment by learning how to conduct ourselves in a wide variety of situations in which persons of deficient or disturbed characters may throw a host of problem behaviors at us. By recognizing their tactics, labeling them correctly, responding to them effectively, and holding the disturbed character accountable for change, anyone can learn the secrets of not being taken advantage of or exploited.

Game Changer: Act Now before It's Too Late

When it comes to relationships with aggressive personalities, you can never give the green light to the conductor of a locomotive that has no brakes. The more aggressive personalities are among the most disturbed in character. It's in their nature to fight often and fight hard for the things they want. They can be inordinately intimidating and hard to resist. Being assertive in relationships with these types of individuals can be a real challenge; but it can definitely be done, especially if you observe the cardinal game changer of acting quickly whenever they begin using their tactics of manipulation and control. One important thing to remember is that these individuals lack internal "brakes," and therefore once they "get rolling," it's hard to put a stop to their behavior. That's why it's so important to respond very quickly with appropriate limit-setting to redefine the terms of engagement.

I remember one couple who came to me for marital counseling. The woman voiced a concern that after her husband had another affair, any sense of trust in their relationship had been seriously eroded. He immediately and forcefully retorted: "Okay, so this is going to be about trashing me and bringing up old news all the time. I thought we were here to get our relationship right. Apparently not…" and went on a long and critical tirade. The woman let him talk for some time and then later, each time she did try and interject a thing or two, he quickly cut her off and had more to say.

As a way of demonstrating the technique of responding quickly and re-establishing the terms of engagement, I asked the woman to sit quietly on the sidelines while I spoke to her husband for a few minutes. When I began to engage him, he made the same forceful attempts to gain the upper hand. The difference was that I was willing to end the interaction immediately upon his first formal attempt to control the process, to suggest he take a time-out in the waiting lounge, and to stop engaging with him at all unless or until he was more willing to engage in an open and equal dialogue. It took several "time-outs" for him to get the message that he wouldn't even get the chance to assert his point of view or sway my opinion (something that means a whole lot to all aggressive characters) unless he observed my rules of engagement. But he finally got the message, and in time the discussion became more even-sided and civil.

The most important thing to remember is how critical it is to act quickly. Sometimes, we don't want to appear too demanding or presumptuous. Sometimes, we just want to afford others the courtesy of having their say. But you can never give the green light to the conductor of a locomotive that has no brakes. Once the train is already chugging down the hill, it has too much momentum built up to try and stop it. By the time it's half-way down the hill, when you try to intervene, you'll get run over.

When dealing with the many different tactics disturbed characters use to manipulate and exploit others, knowing how to respond to each of them better prepares a person to react more quickly. Responding quickly and making clear what the terms of engagement will be are key tools of personal empowerment.

Game Changer: Stay Focused and in the Here and Now

The most powerful aspect of staying focused on the relevant issues and remaining in the here and now is that the spotlight stays centered where it ought to be: on the deficient character and his or her problematic behavior.

Another important game changer when dealing with those who might otherwise manipulate or take advantage of you is to stay focused on the behavior(s) of concern and in the here and now. When you confront a person of deficient or disturbed character about a behavior of concern, they're quite likely to use tactics of evasion or diversion. They'd like to change the subject, divert attention to someone or something else, go back in time, talk about the future, or in some other way get you off track. It's so important to stay focused on the issue(s) at hand despite the other person's best attempts to turn your attention otherwise. It's also important to stay in the here and now as opposed to getting lost in discussions of past events or anticipated future actions.

I once counseled a couple whose stated purpose was to try and heal wounds from several instances of marital infidelity by the wife. During the session, the man brought up that just before the session began, the wife received a phone call from a male with whom she was supposed to have severed ties. When he brought up the issue, she began complaining that he has never forgiven her for the past and began reciting a litany of past accusations and her attempts to reassure him that her behavior had changed. She used a variety of other tactics as well but the result was the same: in a few moments the issue initially at hand fell off the table. The issue was that she entertained a call from a person with whom she was supposed to have severed all relations as a way of rebuilding trust.

In my work with persons in relationships with disturbed characters, I've seen many similar scenarios over the years. Inevitably, those who would otherwise confront their abusers and manipulators end up lost somewhere in the diversionary and other tactics and lose sight of the cycle of abuse being perpetuated in the here and now. Only when they focused on the dynamics in play at the moment and their own role in enabling those dynamics did things begin to change.

The most powerful aspect of staying focused on the relevant issues and remaining in the here and now is that the spotlight stays centered where it ought to be: on the deficient character and his or her problematic behavior. Then there is no running room. And it becomes clearer whether the person has any real motivation to change. If, when duly confronted, the one-time abuser accepts ownership of the behavior in question, expresses genuine remorse for it, and demonstrates over time a willingness not only to repair the damage but to rebuild trust by displaying much different behavior, then you know there is some cause for hope. But none of this is possible unless you're willing to remain focused on behaviors over which you are legitimately concerned and to stay in the here and now when confronting those whose behavior needs to change.

Game Changer: Judge Actions, Not Intentions

Mounds of scientific research attest to the fact that the single best predictor of future behavior is past behavior. That's right. The best indication of whether someone will do something again is if they've done it before. A person's pattern of behavior over time tells us a lot about their level of character development and what we can expect from them in any dealings or relationship we might have.

When I first started out in practice, I was impressed by how many times folks had sought my counseling to help better understand the chronically dysfunctional behavior of someone with whom they were involved. Priding themselves as fairly aware individuals who were familiar with the principles of traditional psychology, they naturally assumed that there must be underlying issues making their partners, co-workers, bosses, etc., behave in troublesome ways. So, they told themselves if they could just understand the underlying reasons for the behavior, they could deal with it better. They also frequently expressed the belief that the other party probably didn't mean to hurt them with their behavior, but must have done so inadvertently out of a misguided attempt to get some personal need met. Such notions were reinforced whenever they confronted the person on problem behavior only to have that person claim that their intentions were misjudged.

While it may sometimes be true that dysfunctional behavior has its roots in unresolved emotional issues and unmet needs, it's the responsibility of the person who has those issues to address and resolve them. It's never the responsibility of others to strive so hard to understand that they ignore, tolerate, or enable the dysfunctional behavior.

Universally, victims of abusive relationships I've counseled began to report an increased sense of personal power and validation once they stopped trying to second-guess why the person mistreating them was doing what they were doing and started holding them accountable for the behavior itself. To do so, they had to stop musing about whether the other person did or did not truly intend to hurt them. In the process, they also became aware of how naturally hesitant they were to ascribe malevolent intentions to others and to seek other more palatable explanations for behavior.

An unfortunate outgrowth of traditional psychology is the popular tendency to look for underlying causes and issues and to second-guess intentions. The presumption is, of course, that most people aren't really aware of all the issues prompting their behavior. Another common presumption is that people wouldn't act in hurtful ways if they weren't dealing with some unmet need, fear, or insecurity underneath. It quickly became a mantra in my work with victims to firmly advocate the principle to "judge actions, not intentions."

Actions speak so much louder than words. It doesn't really matter how loudly a misbehaving person protests that they really didn't mean any harm or that they're being unfairly judged. What matters is that their behavior be allowed to speak for itself. And if it's harmful or destructive behavior, it needs to be confronted, and the person exhibiting it needs to be held accountable for correcting it. Most important, rather than taking on an unwarranted burden to both second-guess the other person's intentions and then try to attend to some presumed underlying need, it's imperative to assess the maturity and integrity of their character by judging their pattern of behavior.

I know so many people who got into destructive relationships in the first place, because, even though they saw the warning signs of problem behaviors, they spent too much mental time and energy guessing about the person's motives. They too often presume that some insecurity, underlying pain, or fear was behind it, and it would disappear with enough love and understanding on their part. By the time they'd begun to question this perspective, they were generally already enmeshed in a bad situation. Adopting the principle of judging actions and not intentions empowers a person to enter relationships in a position of equal advantage, where each person is accountable for their own behavior and their patterns of behavior stand as a testament to their level of character development.

Game Changer: Set Your Limits

A person always loses power when they fail to set and enforce reasonable limits. Setting reasonable and necessary limits is a relationship game changer. There are two types of limits that a person must set in their interpersonal relations if they are to be empowered.

1. Set limits on the kinds of things you are willing to do.

2. Set limit on the kinds of behaviors you will accept from others.

A woman came to my office seeking advice about how to handle some problems she was having with her daughter. I visited with them both together, and key aspects of their relationship became evident within minutes. The mother had just finished making a rather innocuous statement when the daughter blurted out: "That's what you say, you cow!" In response, the mother looked at me and said: "See, that's how she treats me. I've told her to stop being so disrespectful or I won't help her get that car she wants, but she keeps on doing it." I modeled for both of these folks the ground rules I insist on in therapy — that there be no name-calling, demeaning, antagonizing, etc., and I invoked a time out for the session with the proviso that when we resumed, the ground rules would have to be obeyed or there would be another time out. As you might guess, the mother complained that we might never accomplish anything that way. She really didn't see at that point how enabling and reinforcing it was to allow that behavior to repeat itself over and over again— and how ineffective the threat of a future consequence (possibly not financially supporting a car purchase) was in modifying her child's behavior.

I could give literally hundreds of examples, but suffice it to say that people often get themselves into trouble and lose power in their relationships, especially with individuals of deficient or disturbed character when they don't set firm limits both on the behavior that they will tolerate as well as the things they are willing to do to maintain the relationship. In the example I cited, the mother eventually confided that she feared that if she stopped doing all that she was doing that her daughter would think she didn't really love her and she would lose her. She also confided that she didn't feel comfortable with really pulling the plug on her financial support of some of her wishes, because she felt it was her duty to support her and because she hated to see her not have the things most girls want and that her friends had. So, she resorted to threatening to deny her what she never really planned to withhold. In the end, she ended up with virtually no power in the relationship, and her daughter continually ran over her.

Some people can't say "no" easily. Fears of one thing or another (mostly abandonment) keep them from setting limits. What's more, character-disordered personalities, especially the aggressive personalities, don't take the word "no" for an answer. So, there's almost always some kind of hell to pay when you try to set a limit with them. Nonetheless, a person always loses power when they fail to set and enforce reasonable limits. Setting limits is as important as defining and respecting boundaries, and it's a powerful game changer.

Game Changer: Don't Threaten, Just Act

There's no need to "red flag" action that you're willing to take if the disturbed character won't change. Don't threaten, just take action. Another way to remain empowered in your relationships is to avoid threatening to do things while simply taking assertive action on your behalf.

It's common for people to fall into the trap of trying to control the behavior of someone else. This is especially true if the person you're in a relationship with has a deficient or disturbed character. Conscientious people are generally exhausted from all the effort it takes to meet all their responsibilities and make things work in their relationships. The last thing they want is another burden. They hope and pray that the other person will carry their fair share of the load. And, when they don't, they might try and coerce them into behaving better by threatening some action or to leave the relationship altogether. This might result in a temporary manipulation, and the other party might act more responsibly for a while. But in the end, old patterns generally return and the person easily finds himself or herself back in the same old spot.

The tendency to try and coerce another person into right action also has its roots in the common but inaccurate belief that disturbed characters "just don't see what they're doing." So a person can become deluded and think that if they simply maneuver someone into behaving more appropriately, they will eventually "see the light" and change their behavior permanently. But the fact is that disturbed characters know full well what they're doing and how others want them to behave. They know exactly what values and standards persons without disturbances of character hold. They simply don't want to accede to those standards. So there's no need to "red flag" action that you're willing to take on your own behalf if the disturbed character won't change. Your responsibility is to take care of yourself, pure and simple. So, don't threaten action. Take action. Such action doesn't always have to be drastic, but it has to be firm and in your interest. The other party will always get the message that you're not about to be abused, exploited, or manipulated.

Sometimes overly conscientious people equate acting in their own best interest with being selfish. Nothing can be further from the truth. Selfishness is self-absorption, self-seeking behavior that either disregards the rights and needs of others or tramples them deliberately in favor of personal gain. Taking the time and care to tend to your own legitimate wants and needs while not unnecessarily inflicting harm on others (i.e., self-assertion) is perfectly healthy and desirable. That doesn't mean that a good manipulator won't try to convince you that you're somehow doing wrong to take care of yourself. But in your heart, you should know the difference between mistreating someone else and simply taking care of yourself.

If you find yourself dealing with a questionable character, remember your first and foremost responsibility is to take care of yourself. That means action. Don't threaten, cajole, or try to manipulate, just DO. You're more likely to gain the respect of others as well as to increase your own self-respect if you're willing to take assertive action to secure your legitimate needs.

Game Changer: Let Go of Harmful Misconceptions

Our conceptualizations of the situations we find ourselves in cannot only place us at a disadvantage, but can literally harm us. Letting go of harmful misconceptions is a game changer, because it can help you rid yourself of inaccurate ideas about why people behave the way they do and what to do about it. Unfortunately, many of these misconceptions originated with theories about human behavior that were meant to help us understand and deal with one another. Although some of these theories continue to hold some value, some of the most essential tenets of these theories, although widely known and accepted, put us in a position to significantly misjudge situations, especially abusive situations, and end up keeping us in a one-down position when we're trying to understand and deal with the behavior of a disturbed character.

There are so many notions arising out of traditional psychology paradigms that we now know are without merit, some of which seem patently ludicrous to us when we think about them for a moment. For example, we know that children don't become autistic because their mothers were "cold" and non-nurturing during their infancy. We also know that mothers who gave "mixed messages" of love and hate to their infants aren't responsible for the disease of schizophrenia. We know that "bullies" most often aren't really insecure cowards struggling with low self-esteem. We even know that the symptoms and strange events that some of Sigmund Freud's patients reported between themselves and their relatives were more likely signals that they were actually sexual abuse victims as opposed to persons who simply couldn't come to terms with their own lustful urges.

Although it seems like we've come a long way in our thinking, many folks still hold onto traditional notions about the reasons people do the things they do. This wouldn't be so bad if we were only dealing with people who are best described as neurotic to some degree. But we now live in the age of character disturbance. And to change your relationship game with a person of deficient or disordered character, you have to know what really makes them tick. So, when they keep making excuses, lie repeatedly about what they've done, or try to make you feel guilty for confronting them, you have to stop seeing them as insecure, "in denial," or "defending" themselves. Instead, you have to recognize their determination to place themselves above the generally accepted rules or to defy them outright. In short, how we perceive what's going on in an abusive situation will greatly influence how we respond to it. Our conceptualizations of the situations we find ourselves in cannot only place us at a disadvantage but can literally do us harm.

I've received hundreds of emails and testimonials over the years from people who have read my books attesting to the fact that the ultimate "light bulb moment" in a one-time abuse victim's life came when they finally abandoned all the assumptions they had that were rooted in traditional philosophies. For the first time they saw the disturbed character they were dealing with from a more accurate perspective. Their comments are always of similar character: "I see it now"; "I always felt this in my gut but didn't want to believe it"; "Now, I know I'm not crazy after all"; and "Yeah, his self-esteem is out of whack all right but not in the way I once thought." Adopting a new framework for understanding the character they'd been dealing with was not only eye-opening but changes the game. You become empowered, because you come to really understand the tactics of the disturbed character and how to respond to them, no longer falling into the traps to which you used to succumb. When we stop trying to understand it through paradigms created to describe something else and adopt a more accurate framework, everything changes.

Game Changer: Invest Your Energy Where You Have Power

Be sure you invest your time, attention, and emotional energy where you have power. This is a game changer too. One of the critical mistakes people often make, especially if they're dealing with a person of deficient or disordered character, is to focus a lot of time, attention, and energy trying to understand and modify the behavior of the disturbed character. Of course, the behavior of another person is one of many areas of your life where you have no control (i.e., no power). Yet, because persons of defective character will often be good at manipulation and will have you questioning yourself, you can end up spending a lot of time and energy hoping that they will eventually change.

Human beings have one amazing power, but one power only — the power of choice. You have the power to act. You alone command your muscles. You have no power whatsoever over people, places, and things—anything external. Although many entertain the delusion, you have no power over the outcomes of your actions either. You can do everything correctly and still not secure the desired results. Other factors influence that. Naturally, most of the time, unless adverse fate intervenes, if you behave prudently, appropriate rewards follow. But it's important to recognize that nothing external to you is really within your power to control.

The biggest problem people have when they get caught in the trap of trying their best to make a problem relationship work—by focusing time, attention, and energy on the person they can't control—is that they inadvertently discover the behavioral "formula" for depression. Some time ago, researchers discovered that even animals who found themselves in the position of trying everything they could to reach a goal only to find themselves unable to control events, ended up acting helpless. Their "learned helplessness" also led them to display the frustration, anxiety, and eventually the emotional and behavioral "shutdown" that characterizes depression. This helplessness model has been shown to apply to human beings as well. When people invest time and energy trying to make things happen only to find that no matter what they do or try nothing seems to change, they end up feeling frustrated, anxious, despondent, angry, helpless, and depressed.

Fortunately, there is also a behavioral formula for vitality, joy, and satisfaction. That formula is to invest your time, attention, and emotional energy where you have power: your power to act. In addition to having counseled hundreds of individuals whose character needed much in the way of social development, I've also counseled hundreds of individuals who have been victims of abusive, manipulative, and exploitative relationships. Most of the victims were to some degree depressed when they first came to see me and always for the same reason. They had invested considerable time and energy trying to understand their abuser, trying to make the relationship work, trying to maintain hope that the other person's behavior would eventually change. They'd tell me things like: "I know he must have low self-esteem to be acting like this, and I know that once he realizes how much he is loved his wounds will eventually heal." Clearly, harmful conceptualizations about the reasons for the problems, and misdirected energy, had only succeeded in putting these individuals in a position to remain mired in a destructive relationship and to become quite depressed in the process.

Here is Ellen's (name and significant details altered) story who, after years of anguish, discovered the tools of personal empowerment.

> I feel more alive today because I know I have power. I know all the tactics by heart. I know what some people are really like — how they think and how they act. I know what to expect and how to respond. But most of all, I know that I can set the rules. I know that I have a choice and I can decide what the limits and boundaries are. I don't have to be satisfied with only praying for change, I can do something. Don't worry, I'm never going to be the steamroller my partner was with me. But I am committed to taking better care of myself. I will never go back to the way it was.

***

There's no way to see how the game changers work than reading the words of Ellen. She decided to invest her time, attention, and energy where she had power. She traded depression for joy and being a doormat existence for asserting herself. She understands all the principles and tools. I doubt that she'll ever be a victim again.

I'm going to end this book as I began. Are you happy? What would it take for you to be truly happy in your relationships? Are you willing to face up to the issues and seek change? Are you ready to give up on ever find a fulfilling relationship? You don't have to just "settle." Disturbed characters don't have to remain a conundrum. Change the terms of engagement; change your game.

Take Away

Change your game. You don't have to settle for how things are; and you certainly don't have to be a victim of disturbed characters. When someone engages in a behavior that's a problem, the reason they do it is irrelevant. If we try too hard to understand the behavior, before long we'll find ourselves excusing it and eventually enabling it.

Empowerment Tools

Keys to personal empowerment:

1. Recognize the pitfalls of traditionally-accepted explanations for why people do the things they do.

2. Adopt a new framework for understanding the underpinnings of behavior — especially the behavior of individuals of deficient or disturbed character.

Game Changers:

1. Accept no excuses.

2. Act now before it's too late.

3. Stay focused and in the here and now.

4. Judge actions, not intentions.

5. Set your limits.

6. Don't threaten, just act.

7. Invest your energy where you have power.

About the Authors

George K. Simon Jr., Ph.D. is the leading expert on manipulators and other disturbed characters. He knows how they push your buttons and get the better of you and why, despite all the thing you've tried, nothing seems to work. Dr. Simon is not only an author, but a public speaker, consultant, professional trainer, and composer who has appeared on numerous national, regional, and local television and radio programs. His book *In Sheep's Clothing: Understanding and Dealing with Manipulative People* is an international bestseller, published in several foreign languages, and has been nearing twenty years in print. It consistently draws praise from readers who want to understand the difficult people in their lives and deal with them more effectively. He believes firmly in the vital relationship between freedom and personal responsibility, and is deeply concerned about the character crisis plaguing Western civilization and eroding the greatness of America.

Dr. Simon has given over three-hundred professional and public workshops and/or training seminars. And he has consulted with numerous professional agencies, institutions, and companies. His work is also featured on several popular online resources providing information on disturbances of character and other psychological issues. Find him on the very popular blog www.manipulative-people.com. Or find him at his website www.drgeorgesimon.com, or the international blog, *Psychology, Philosophy, and Real Life* at www.counsellingresource.com, where he is a major contributing author. You can also read his insightful contributions on this blog's "Ask the Psychologist" feature.

Dr. Simon's first book, *In Sheep's Clothing: Understanding and Dealing with Manipulative People* has enjoyed unprecedented bestseller status and is regarded by many as the definitive manual for understanding manipulative and other problem characters. Human-Nature.com ranked this book as the eleventh bestselling book of all time in the area of psychiatry, and among the top one-hundred in categories such as self-help, psychology, self-improvement, and human relations. In this book Dr. Simon uncovers the tactics manipulators use to deceive and get the better of others. He explains how to avoid being victimized and how to be more empowered in any relationship.

In *Character Disturbance*, Dr. Simon provides an in-depth but understandable explanation for the most difficult and problematic personalities in your life and the special precautions and necessary perspective you need to take to keep from being victimized by them. Ever wonder whether it's just you or the whole world has in fact gone crazy? This book explains "the phenomenon of our time," the reasons for the character crisis we face, and the necessary steps society must take to restore sanity to our lives. It also provides a much needed guide to what to look for when seeking help for dealing with the disturbed characters in your life.

Dr. Simon's first book specifically geared for Christian readers, *The Judas Syndrome,* is available from Amazon.com. This book explains the major reasons why bad things happen in life and provides powerful vignettes that demonstrate the power of faith to save us from our baser selves.

Dr. Simon's books are readily available at Amazon.com and all the major online booksellers. They're also available at most bookstores. Bulk orders are available at a discount from the publishers.

Composed at the turn of the new millennium, *America, My Home!* is the first genuinely patriotic anthem in nearly twenty years. Debuted to a cheering crowd of 10,000 on Memorial Day, 2000, the song gained popularity when a regional television station aired it along with a video montage after the attacks of 9/11, and has since been performed in various venues to audiences totaling over one million. While working on a book on the interdependence of character and freedom, Dr. George Simon experienced a rekindling of his own patriotic spirit. He scored a melody that had been haunting him for nearly seven years, and, together with his wife Dr. Sherry Simon, penned the straight-from-the-heart lyrics. Hear for yourself why so many say that the song is one of their favorites. Visit https://www.youtube.com/user/georgeksimon.

Dr. Simon also hosts a weekly broadcast on UCY.TV called *Character Matters*. Tune in on Sunday evenings at 7 p.m. Eastern to ask a question or share an experience. Avail yourself of his years of experience dealing with disturbed and disordered characters.

M. Kathryn Armistead, Ph.D. is a Nashville-based writer. Her Ph.D. in Religion and Personality is from Vanderbilt University. Dr. Armistead is the author, ghostwriter, or editor of more than two-hundred books. She helps writers craft marketable books and write with clarity and purpose. Some of her own books include: *Wesleyan Theology and Social Science: The Dance of Practical Divinity and Discovery*, (edited by M. Kathryn Armistead, Brad Strawn, and Ron Wright, Cambridge Scholars Press, 2010); and *God-Images in the Healing Process* (Fortress Press, Minneapolis, 1995). To find her go to www.kathyarmistead.com.

Appendix
Helpful Distinctions and Definitions

Because there are so many misconceptions and confusion over key psychological terms, here are some distinctions that are helpful in learning the art of healthy confrontation.

Anxiety Disorders

Four of the more commonly diagnosed conditions include:

Phobia. A phobia is when excessive or irrational and uncontrolled anxiety is attached to an identifiable stressor, either social or object or situation-specific (e.g., fear of crowds, high places, certain animals, public speaking, etc.). And people who suffer from phobias will generally go to great lengths to avoid exposing themselves to the circumstances that give rise to anxiety.

Panic. People with this condition experience "attacks" of extreme anxiety. These episodes are sometimes triggered by particular circumstances. But they can also appear "out of the clear blue sky" and without warning, often adding to a person's distress. As with phobias, individuals who suffer from panic often begin to avoid placing themselves in circumstances in which they fear panic symptoms might occur. And sometimes this can lead to them avoiding many social and occupational situations that are essential to their overall welfare.

Obsessive-Compulsive Disorder (OCD). Obsessions are intrusive thoughts that are sometimes irrational and excessive yet hard for a person afflicted with them to shake off. Compulsions, on the other hand, are strong urges to engage in certain actions or perform certain ritualistic behaviors. Obsessions and compulsions can engender anxiety in themselves. But more often, individuals with OCD engage in their compulsive habits or mental fixations to stave off even higher levels of anxiety.

Post-Traumatic Stress Disorder (PTSD). PTSD is an often misunderstood condition. It's not simply experiencing the understandable mixed emotions that follow a painful circumstance. Rather, folks that suffer from PTSD have experienced a life-threatening or severely traumatic event and often have recurring bouts of anxiety following that event. They also might have "flashbacks" of the traumatizing experience, anxiety, and avoidance associated with situations or circumstances that in some way are reminiscent of the trauma, and a variety of other symptoms including emotional instability, difficulty sleeping and nightmares, depression, uncharacteristic behavior, and a lowered threshold for stress tolerance.

Assertive vs. Aggressive Behavior

Assertive Behavior

1. Fights fair, i.e., without putting the other at a disadvantage.

2. Fights for a legitimate purpose.

3. Fights with discipline, by using self-imposing limits designed to prevent undue harm to another.

4. Is always non-violent.

5. Fights constructively, i.e., with the goal of improving a situation for all concerned.

1. Seeks unfair advantage and attempts to victimize another.

2. Fights for self-serving and possible immoral purposes.

3. Fight without limits or with poor limits on that the person is willing to say and/or do—a "win at all costs" attitude.

4. Is sometimes violent.

5. Fights in a destructive manner, i.e., in a manner that destroys opportunities to improve a situation for all concerned.

Character

The word "character" derives from both the Old French and Greek words meaning to engrave or furrow a *distinctive mark*. The word has been used to denote the most distinguishing traits of overall personality that uniquely define or "mark" an individual as a social being. Most especially, the term commonly reflects an individual's positive personality aspects—those socially desirable qualities and virtues such as self-control, ethical behavior, loyalty, and fortitude.

Contrition

Contrition is a poorly understood concept despite how essential it is to repairing damage in relationships. The term comes from a Latin word meaning "crushed." The contrite person feels crushed in spirit —crushed under the weight of their own moral deficiency. And the contrite person recognizes and accepts the work it might take to rebuild a sense of self they can live with. You know contrition is genuine by the actions a person takes. The contrite individual 1) doesn't make excuses, minimize, justify, or try to save face but humbly acknowledges their failures and shortcomings and sincerely strives to make amends, and 2) makes genuine and sustained efforts to not only to do better in the future but also to be a better person. Contrition is much more than saying you're sorry or appearing sorrowful. It's proving through your actions that you really are sorry and working hard not to find yourself feeling sorry for the exact same failure in the future.

Defense Mechanisms

Defense mechanisms are an unconscious intra-psychic processes that help individuals alleviate the anxiety and emotional pain associated with conflict, usually thought to be between their primal urges and their conscious. The reason neurotic individuals develop problematic symptoms is because these unconscious tools of anxiety mitigation, as powerful as they are, are neither adequate nor fully adaptive. Neurotic people often seek help because their defenses have become increasingly inadequate or have begun to break down, letting the underlying pain rise to the surface.

Disordered characters engage in certain behaviors so "automatic" that it's tempting to thing they do them unconsciously. On the surface, these behaviors often so resemble defense mechanisms that they can be misinterpreted as such, especially by individuals overly immersed in traditional paradigms. However many of these behaviors are more accurately regarded as tactics of manipulation, impression-management, and responsibility-resistance.

Dissociation and Compartmentalization

There's another phenomenon frequently confused with dissociation: compartmentalization. Individuals with psychopathic traits come in two main varieties: those with a markedly deficient or totally absent capacity for human empathy, and those who have some empathy capacity but also have a special capacity to wall-off or "compartmentalize" any emotion when they're in a predatory behavior mode (i.e., when they intend to victimize). And mistaking compartmentalization for dissociation is one of the main reasons why some folks fail to recognize the warning signs of psychopathy.

Dissociation and Just Not Caring

Callous disregard for others and important social norms, in its many destructive forms, is sometimes perceived erroneously as an example of dissociation. It can also be erroneously perceived as attention deficiency or even unconscious behavior. Stanton Samenow was among the first to note that many disturbed characters pay attention to the things to which they want to pay attention and "selectively" filter out of their awareness those things that don't particularly matter to them. **It's not that they're unaware, it's that they just don't care.** How your behavior impacts others has to matter to you if you're going to be particularly mindful of it. And many disturbed characters among us simply don't care enough about the things we want them to care about to pay much attention to them. While they seem oblivious and even detached at times, most of the time they simply don't care to be mindful. And their lack of mindfulness is a conscious, deliberate choice, whereas dissociation is an unconscious mental defense against unbearable emotional pain. They're too dedicated to fulfilling their own selfish desires to care much about how others might be impacted.

Distortion and Denial

Just as deliberate disregard is not dissociation, deliberate distortion is not the same as denial. A person in a true state of denial is dealing with an emotional reality so painful that primitive unconscious mechanisms kick in order to prevent their conscious mind from experiencing it. Denial is not the same as stubbornly refusing to admit the obvious. It's also not the same as kidding yourself about the truth of things. In short, denial is not conscious lying but rather unconscious protection against unbearable pain. However, a person can make a habit of deceiving and distorting. But that doesn't mean they're in denial or can't readily recognize the truth. It just means they're not of a mind to acknowledge what they know to be true unless someone holds their feet to the fire.

Disturbance and Disorder

Not all problematic aspects of personality or character rise to the level of a true disorder. For a disturbance of personality and/or character to be considered a disorder, it must be of such intensity, inflexibility, and intractability that it impairs adaptive functioning in a wide variety of situations.

Guilt and Shame

Guilt is feeling bad about something you've done, whereas shame is feeling bad about who you are. The popular wisdom for some time has been that guilt is both essential and often helpful to moral functioning, but shame is to be avoided, because it is counterproductive at best or toxic at worst. Some folks have extended the meaning of shame to include feelings of humiliation, embarrassment, or disgrace. But shame is not synonymous with any of these things. And only recently have some researchers bucked the long popular trend by presenting evidence that some shame can indeed be good. When we appraise ourselves as lacking in some way, especially with respect to the integrity and solidity of our character, it can be an occasion for us to renew a commitment not just to do better but to be better.

Neurosis and Character Disturbance

Neurosis and character disturbance are at opposite poles of a continuum, with each individual personality falling somewhere along the continuum; therefore, character disturbance is always a matter of degree. Just as we've come to learn that autistic conditions exist along a continuum (the official classification now carrying the label Autism Spectrum Disorder), character disturbances exist not only on a continuum of intensity and severity but also on a spectrum that reflects the relative presence of what has been long called "neurosis," as opposed to pure character pathology. Very few individuals are virtually devoid of any neurosis or are severely character disordered. Most folks lie somewhere along a continuum that reflects varying degrees of neurosis vs. character disturbance.

When a neurotic person seeks counseling, you can safely assume that there are some emotional issues that need to be attended to or resolved. Perhaps their feelings have been long repressed. Perhaps their feelings are very mixed and conflicted, in which case they are likely to be engendering a fair degree of anxiety. In any case, helping a person to more intimately connect with their feelings and sort through their troubled emotions is the hallmark of the traditional psychotherapy. Regardless of the problems he is having, therapy for the neurotic almost always involves considerable focus on feelings.

The problems the disturbed character has functioning well in a social context are not so much a consequence of the way he feels but the way he thinks.

In contrast, the problems the disturbed character has functioning well in a social context are not so much a consequence of the way he feels but the way he thinks. It's the ill-gotten attitudes, distorted thinking patterns, and dysfunctional core beliefs he has come to hold that are the main causes of problems. In recent years, awareness of this fact has spurred a revolution in therapeutic approaches. The term "cognitive-behavioral therapy" refers to an orientation founded on the principle that there is an inextricable connection between a person's core beliefs, attitudes, and thinking patterns, and his or her behavior. For example, if a man's core beliefs include the notions that a woman is naturally inferior to any man, is destined by nature to be submissive to males, is a rightful personal possession if she should become involved in a serious relationship with him, and has value to him primarily as an object of sexual gratification, one would not be particularly surprised to learn that this man had a history of abusive conduct with his wife or girlfriend. How we think in large measure determines how we will act. When dealing with disordered characters, the kinds of problematic thinking they habitually engage in is a much bigger issue to address as opposed to how they are feeling about anything. Once distorted thinking patterns are successfully challenged and corrected, problems might actually become resolved altogether. If there are still emotional issues to address, they certainly can be dealt with, but only after the character issues and the distorted thinking pattern responsible for them have been resolved.

Personality

Personality can be defined as an individual's preferred style of perceiving, thinking about, and interacting with others, self, and the world at large. Factors that contribute to the development of personality include biological predispositions, environmental factors, and the dynamic interplay between biology and the environment. Those aspects of an individual's personality that reflect their capacity for and commitment to virtuous and meritorious conduct define a person's character. The aggressive personalities are individuals whose overall style of interacting involves considerable, persistent, maladaptive aggression expressed in a variety of ways and in a wide range of circumstances.

Regret

Regret is the unpleasant emotional response (generally, sadness or unhappiness) we have to an external event or circumstance. It comes from a French word meaning to "complain" or "lament." You can have regret about not being able to attend an event because of a prior commitment. You can also regret an unfortunate happenstance, a bad stroke of luck, or disappointing turn of events. You can even have regret for a situation that arises purely as a consequence of your own behavior. But in any case, the regret response is a purely "amoral" one. That is, feelings of regret have nothing to do with the perceived moral rightness or wrongness of anything. Rather, regret is only about the displeasure you feel about the circumstance itself and the negative impact it may have on you.

Remorse

Remorse is different from regret. Remorse is the experience of deep anguish over something you've done that has created a bad circumstance or caused injury to others (whether that injury was intended or unintended). The word comes from a Latin word meaning "to bite with more force," and refers the gnawing feeling or gnashing of teeth a person of conscience who knows they have done wrong might experience. It's a moral response to a moral failure and as such, it arises out of a sense of guilt.

21036004R00104

Printed in Great Britain
by Amazon